Job

Job

The Cry of the Righteous Sufferer

Benjamin Gum

SOUL PURPOSE PUBLISHING
Books & Music

Copyright © 2021 Benjamin Gum
All rights reserved.
ISBN 978-1-7344962-6-0

Soul Purpose Publishing
Shawnee, KS

Unless otherwise noted, all Scripture quotations are taken from the Christian Standard Bible®, copyright © 2017 by Holman Bible Publishers. Used by permission. Christian Standard Bible® and CSB® are federally registered trademarks of Holman Bible Publishers.

Contents

LESSON 1 OVERVIEW & PROLOGUE: JOB'S INTEGRITY, BLESSING & INTERCESSION (CH.1, VV.1-5) 1
- OVERVIEW 1
- JOB'S INTEGRITY 4
- JOB'S BLESSING 5
- JOB'S INTERCESSION 6

LESSON 2 PROLOGUE: JOB'S HUMILIATION BY SATAN – TEST ONE (CH.1, VV.6 - 22) 7
- GOD'S SOVEREIGN RULE, THE COUNCIL AND THE OPPONENT 7
- THE CHALLENGE 7
- TEST ONE: EVERYTHING HE OWNS 9
- THE RESULTS 10

LESSON 3 PROLOGUE: JOB'S HUMILIATION BY SATAN – TEST TWO (CH.2) 13
- GOD'S (STILL) SOVEREIGN RULE, THE COUNCIL AND THE OPPONENT (AGAIN) 13
- THE SECOND CHALLENGE 14
- SATAN'S THEOLOGY 15
- TEST TWO: ALL BUT HIS LIFE 16
- THE RESULTS 17
- JOB'S THREE FRIENDS 18
- REFLECTION 19

LESSON 4 DIALOGUE: JOB'S LAMENT (CH.3) 21
- JOB'S RESTRAINT 21
- JOB'S LAMENT 21
    - *Cursing His Day* 23
    - *Cursing His Birth* 24
    - *Questioning and the "Thing" Job Fears* 25
- REFLECTION 27

LESSON 5 DIALOGUE: ROUND ONE: ELIPHAZ V. JOB (CHS.4 - 7) 29
- ELIPHAZ'S REBUKE 29
    - *The Friend's Limited Perspective* 29
    - *Retribution Theology* 30
    - *From Sympathy to Judgment* 30
    - *Expert Advice* 33
- JOB'S RESPONSE 36
    - *His Devastation* 36
    - *His Friends* 37
    - *His Righteousness* 38
    - *God's Target?* 40
- REFLECTION ON THE FIRST EXCHANGE 42

LESSON 6 DIALOGUE: ROUND ONE: BILDAD V. JOB (CHS.8 - 10) 43

- Bildad's Judgment 43
  - *Presumptions* 43
  - *Historical Evidence* 44
  - *Bittersweet Prediction* 45
- Job's Response 46
  - *The Impossible Appeal* 46
  - *A Possibility* 48
  - *The Hopeless Defense* 49
  - *The Missing Mediator* 50
  - *The Appeal (Anyway)* 50
  - *Reflection on the Second Exchange* 52

LESSON 7 DIALOGUE: ROUND ONE: ZOPHAR V. JOB (CHS.11 - 14) 53
- Zophar's Assessment 53
  - *Shock (Zophar's, and probably ours)* 53
  - *Advice* 54
- Job's Response 56
  - *Sarcasm and His Own Shock* 56
  - *Common Knowledge* 56
  - *The Preferred Appeal* 58
  - *Risk and Hope* 59
  - *Job's Prayer* 59
  - *Gospel Cravings* 62

LESSON 8 DIALOGUE: ROUND TWO: ELIPHAZ V. JOB (CHS.15 - 17) 63
- Eliphaz Gets More Direct 63
  - *Questioning that Threatens* 64
  - *Threatening Questions* 66
  - *Warnings About the Wicked (Read: Job)* 67
- Job Responds 68
  - *Trading Places* 68
  - *Targeted by God and the Wicked* 69
  - *A Speck of Hope Wrapped in Despair* 70
  - *Security, Scorn and Strength* 71

LESSON 9 DIALOGUE: ROUND TWO: BILDAD V. JOB (CHS.18 - 19) 75
- Bildad Gets Even More Indignant 75
  - *Who Do You Think You Are?* 75
  - *The Wicked and Unjust Man* 76
- Job Fires Back 78
  - *It's Not About You* 78
  - *God Has Wronged Me* 78
  - *Have Mercy* 80
  - *Job's Great and Only Hope (and Ours)* 80
  - *Reflection on Seeing the Redeemer* 84

LESSON 10 DIALOGUE: ROUND TWO: ZOPHAR V. JOB (CHS.20 - 21) 85
ZOPHAR TRIES AGAIN 85
Unsettling Thoughts and Insults 85
The Wicked Person's Lot from God 85
JOB RESPONDS 88
Bearing and Mocking 88
Why Shouldn't I Be Impatient? 88
This Life Does Not Reveal God's Justice (Always or Fully) 91

LESSON 11 DIALOGUE: ROUND THREE: ELIPHAZ V. JOB (CHS.22 - 24) 95
ELIPHAZ'S LAST REBUKE 95
No Difference to God 95
Job's Injustice Upon Others 96
Come to Terms with God 97
JOB'S REPLY 99
If Only… 99
I Cannot Perceive Him 100
Yet He Knows 100
What He Has Decreed for Me 101
Why? 102
Reflection on Testing as Proving 104

LESSON 12 DIALOGUE: ROUND THREE: BILDAD V. JOB (CHS.25 - 27) 105
BILDAD'S LAST BRIEF BARRAGE 105
Out of Blows 105
Power and Purity 105
JOB'S "HAYMAKER" 108
Back Atcha (Sarcasm Again) 108
Whispers of God's Greatness 108
Job's Oath 109
Job's Curse 110
The Wicked Man's Lot 111
GOSPEL REALITIES 112

LESSON 13 DIALOGUE: JOB'S HYMN TO WISDOM AND CLOSING STATEMENT (CHS.28 - 31) 115
HYMN TO WISDOM 115
The Miner and Earthly Treasures 115
The Value and Elusiveness of Wisdom 116
The Source for Wisdom 117
JOB'S CLOSING STATEMENT 118
The Good Ol' Days 118
These Days of Suffering 120
One Last Protest of Innocence 124
Reflection 127

LESSON 14 DIALOGUE: ELIHU'S SPEECHES 1 & 2 (CHS.32 - 34) 129
    Eli-who? the Angry Youngster 129
    Elihu's First Speech 131
        "I must speak" 131
        "Refute me if you can" 133
        "You are wrong in this matter" 134
        "God disciplines and restores" 134
    Elihu's Second Speech 136
        "Let us judge for ourselves…" 137
        "Could one who hates justice govern the world?" 139
        "God does not need to examine a person…in court." 140
        "When God is silent" 141
        "Suppose someone says" 141
        Reflection 142

LESSON 15 DIALOGUE: ELIHU'S SPEECHES 3 & 4 (CHS.35 - 37) 143
    Elihu's Third Speech 143
        "If you are righteous, what do you give him?" 143
        "God does not listen to empty cries" 144
    Elihu's Fourth Speech 144
        "I will ascribe justice to my Maker" 145
        "God instructs them by their torment" 145
        "You have been tested by affliction" 146
        "God is exalted, and you should praise his work" 146
        "Stop and consider God's wonders" 148

LESSON 16 DIALOGUE: JOB'S HUMILIATION BY GOD, ROUND ONE (CH.38 – CH.40, V.5) 151
    Different Kinds of Humiliation 151
    Bookends to the Dialogue 152
    The LORD's First Speech 152
        From the Whirlwind 152
        Answering with Questions 152
        "Who is this…?" 153
        "Where were you…?" 153
        "Do you know…?" 154
        "Will you correct the Almighty?" 158
    Job's First Response: Humble Silence 159

LESSON 17 DIALOGUE: JOB'S HUMILIATION BY GOD, ROUND TWO (CH.40, V6 – CH.42, V.6) 163
    The LORD's Second Speech 163
        "Would you really challenge my justice?" 163
        "Your own right hand can deliver you." 163
        "Can anyone capture Behemoth?" 164
        "Can you pull in Leviathan with a hook?" 165
    Job's Second Response: Confession and Repentance 168

LESSON 18 EPILOGUE: JOB'S INTEGRITY, INTERCESSION AND GREATER BLESSING (CH.42, VV.7 - 17) 171
   Job's Integrity Vindicated by the LORD 171
      "...the truth about me..." *172*
      "...my servant Job..." *174*
   Job's Intercession for His Friends 174
   Job's Greater Blessing 175
   Reflection Upon the Lessons from Job 177

ABOUT THE AUTHOR 179

Acknowledgements

Acknowledgement seems too small a word to express thanks to the God through whom and for whose glory this study has been written. It is this writer's aim to keep Job's ultimate lesson in mind: God is enough! It is enough that he knows me, has called me and has redeemed me. To participate in his work to enrich lives through his gospel is a surpassing privilege. To expose the beautiful ways he has preached this gospel in one of the oldest Bible stories is a joy.

I owe no greater earthly debt than to my wife, Dawna, who has encouraged me in developing this study and who has helped me refine it even while we have both celebrated what God has taught us through it. Thanks so much, honey, for all the ways you sharpen me!

Thanks too for those in our small groups who have walked through this study with us: Tim and Nicole Houser, Doug and Nancy Carlson, Wil and Kathy Castro and Linda Wilson. You have brought new thoughts and insights to mind with your discussions and reflections. And, sometimes you've even offered your services as a volunteer editing and proofing staff! You have been a great joy and encouragement as we see God bless this work.

All the glory to the Almighty, our glorious Redeemer!

Dedication

This study is offered to all who are suffering in so many ways and for so many reasons. It is especially dedicated with compassion for those who have suffered personal hardship and who have lost loved ones in the Covid-19 pandemic that rocked our world in 2020 and beyond. It continues to be a trying time for all, and we Christians are suffering too, but we may be refreshed from a well of hope from which so many cannot draw. May we all through his Spirit, his Word and our prayers navigate these times of confusion and calamity clinging like Job to that One who is our Hope. May the world see and hear and be drawn to life by our testimony: our Redeemer lives, and we know we will one day see him in our flesh, and not as a stranger. May our hearts long for him!

Introduction

For centuries the person Job has been a touchstone for people going through tough times. Drawing from his story, many counselors have offered much advice. *God is still there even when you don't feel him or hear from him. God is big enough to handle your questions, your frustrations, and even your rants. We don't always understand what God is doing, and we don't have the whole picture.*

These are all true, and they are applications from this text. But if we dig deeper and look closely – even in the long dramatic speeches of the dialogue sections – we will find that this book reveals gospel cravings. This story reveals a cry that we find familiar and not just because we suffer too. We share common ground with Job not only in what we cry *from* but also what we cry *for*. When we don't understand and don't have answers, we cry out for more than just to be heard. We cry out to be rescued. In the suffocating seasons of suffering we are especially aware that we need a Mediator. Job wants answers, to be sure, but his greater cry is for his Redeemer. In the end, he will find this Redeemer to be his greatest need and his only satisfaction.

So, while this story deals a lot with theology – what people believe about God – it turns out to be much more than theological. It is personal. Job's suffering brings him to crave a personal encounter with God. He will cry for God to show up, and when he finally does, Job will find that all he really needs is the utterly incomprehensible power and majesty and mercy of the Almighty. When life falls apart, when friends and family are no help, or worse, are antagonistic, Job clings to a personal hope in the God he trusts. God does not disappoint. We too can have no other hope, and in Christ we too find that God does not disappoint. For whenever we cry out from our unprovoked suffering we look to the One who suffered the worst injustice for us, Jesus.

As we walk with Job from blessing to suffering through craving to renewal, let us reflect on our own lives and be reminded that we serve the same God. Let us express our own confident hope along with Job:

> Even after my skin has been destroyed,
> yet I will see God in my flesh.
> I will see him myself;
> my eyes will look at him, and not as a stranger.
> My heart longs within me.

Lesson 1 Overview & Prologue: Job's Integrity, Blessing & Intercession (Ch.1, Vv.1-5)

Opening Discussion
When have you experienced hardship you didn't feel you had brought on yourself? How did it feel, what did you think, and how did you react?

Overview
Before we can begin to understand the message of this book, we need to do some prep work. Here is background information and an important overview of Job's purposes, themes, and implications.

"Job"
The name Job means "hated" or "much persecuted." Etymologically the name Job could be related to the Hebrew word for "enemy."[1] [It] is derived from an Arabic word signifying *repentance*.[2] (cf. 42:6) The prophet Ezekiel mentions Job along with Noah and Daniel, and this seems to imply that he took Job as a real person. This is also the implication of James 5:11:[3]

Historical setting
Job appears to be set in ancient pre-Israel, an Eastern setting with Semitic names. Though the story of Job has its setting outside Israel to the east and south (Uz is related to Edom, which may be the setting of the book, cf. 2:11; 6:19; Lam. 4:21), the author of Job is a Hebrew, thoroughly immersed in the Hebrew Scriptures (see below).[4]

Genre
Job is Old Testament (OT) Wisdom Literature offered in a blend of historical narrative, lawsuit, lament, and poetry. The book of Job is an astonishing mixture of almost every kind of literature to be found in the Old Testament.[5] In *genre* Job stands closest to the epic history of early Israel, which found its golden expression in the patriarchal stories, the saga of the exodus, the career of David, the tale of Ruth.[6] Some ancient works have bits of similar content, but Job is largely unique. In form, the dialogues in Job resemble "contest" literature of the ancient Near East (for example,

---

[1] Crossway Bibles. (2008). *The ESV Study Bible* (p. 869). Wheaton, IL: Crossway Bibles.
[2] Jamieson, R., Fausset, A. R., & Brown, D. (1997). *Commentary Critical and Explanatory on the Whole Bible* (Vol. 1, p. 308). Oak Harbor, WA: Logos Research Systems, Inc.
[3] Crossway Bibles. (2008). *The ESV Study Bible* (p. 871). Wheaton, IL: Crossway Bibles.
[4] Crossway Bibles. (2008). *The ESV Study Bible* (p. 869). Wheaton, IL: Crossway Bibles.
[5] Andersen, F. I. (1976). *Job: An Introduction and Commentary* (Vol. 14, p. 34). Downers Grove, IL: InterVarsity Press.
[6] Andersen, F. I. (1976). *Job: An Introduction and Commentary* (Vol. 14, p. 38). Downers Grove, IL: InterVarsity Press.

Job: The Cry of the Righteous Sufferer

"The Babylonian Theodicy"). The literature of the ancient Near East has not yielded another 'Job'. There is a considerable list of writings from this region, and a few from further afield, which remind one of Job in this way or that. But none comes close to Job when each work is examined as a whole. Each shows more differences than similarities, and not one can be considered seriously as a possible source or model for Job.[7] Irony is a key component of this literary work.

Date

The *events* recorded in Job probably occur between Abraham's day and the 2nd century BC, probably during the patriarchal period, given Job's lifespan extended 140 years after these events. The dating of the *writing* is difficult, since it seems (intentionally) disconnected from ancient Israelite historical markers like Abraham, the Exodus, the Kingdom Era, or the exile. It seems likely to have been written down sometime between Moses and Ezra, but the traditional view holds that the writing was near the events, so probably during the patriarchal period.

The earliest reference to Job outside the book itself is in Ezekiel. The prophet names three paragons of virtue: Noah, Daniel, and Job (Ezek. 14:14, 20). It is not certain whether Ezekiel knew of these men from the biblical narrative or from other traditions; this is particularly true for Daniel, a book that could not have been complete in Ezekiel's day. If Ezekiel knew of Job through the biblical book, then it would be preexilic.[8]

Writer

This work is anonymous. Traditional theories about authorship include Moses and Solomon among many others, including Job himself.

Purpose

The book of Job works in concert with other biblical *wisdom literature* to wrestle with the problem of suffering, especially the suffering of the righteous. It shows that God's sovereign rule is above our pay grade. It reveals the great gap between God's sovereign activity and man's limited information. It shows that God is in the driver's seat, not man, not our opponents. It calls for continued trust in God, based in a hope of Someone to mediate for us, a Redeemer, and based on the hope of ultimate blessing.

Major Themes

INTEGRITY and MEDIATION – The story displays God's absolute integrity against man's imperfect integrity so that we yearn for a perfect Man to intercede for us. The irony is that God describes Job as having integrity, while Satan's accusation and Job's confusion implies God might *not* have integrity. The man Job fails to some extent (and his wife and friends even worse), but God still gives blessing based on the coming Man who will *not* fail.

---

[7] Andersen, F. I. (1976). Job: An Introduction and Commentary (Vol. 14, p. 33). Downers Grove, IL: InterVarsity Press.
[8] Crossway Bibles. (2008). *The ESV Study Bible* (p. 869). Wheaton, IL: Crossway Bibles.

Overview & Job's Integrity, Blessing & Intercession

SUFFERING and HUMILIATION – The story shows Job as a type of the coming Christ, who would supremely suffer the wrath of God unjustly to appropriate a "happy ending" for all who unite with him by faith. Job's suffering refines and perfects him; Christ's suffering refines and perfects all saints. Job is humbled by Satan and by God. Christ humbled himself for our sake so we might be lifted up with him.

GOD'S ABSOLUTE SOVEREIGNTY and BLESSING – God rules as all-powerful, all-wise and perfectly just. All blessing comes from his generosity whom he may rightly show to anyone. This is contrasted with man's limited perspective and faulty assessments. Job's friends cannot know what Job knows – that he has done nothing to bring calamity upon himself. Job does not know what the reader knows – the heavenly purpose behind the tests. God's sovereignty is also contrasted with the limited power of our opponent, Satan.

HOPE and TRUST – Job is not given an explanation for his calamity but looks forward with hope and clings to God.

Worldview Correctives
NATURALISM/MATERIALISM - There is plenty going on in the supernatural/spiritual realm.
POLYTHEISM - There is only one God here.
DEISM - God is watching and active.
DUALISM - Satan can do nothing without permission. He is not pitted against God as an equal power.
RETRIBUTION THEOLOGY/PROSPERITY THEOLOGY – Every blessing is a result of God's generous choice. He is not obligated by our best efforts, nor is suffering always a sure sign of punishment.

Interpretive biblical cross-references
How do other biblical writers understand, interpret and apply Job?
Ezek 14:12-14 - Job is given as an example of righteousness but as an insufficient intercessor.
Jas 5:11 - Job is given as an example of endurance through suffering, with integrity of speech and looking forward to blessing.

Summary: Other biblical writers interpret Job as a story of God's compassion and mercy shown to the righteous who endure suffering with integrity while they wait for a perfect Intercessor who brings God's blessing.

Job: The Cry of the Righteous Sufferer

Discussion
If you have ever studied Job, what has been your biggest takeaway from the story or the book?

Does awareness of satanic activity affect your day-to-day living? If so, how?

Have you heard others reject God because of bad things that happen to them or others (the classic "problem of evil")? How did you or might you respond to their questions and objections?

How does a statement like "I know that my Redeemer lives" impact your thinking when things are falling apart?

Job's Integrity
Who would you describe as a person of integrity? Who would you say has no integrity at all? What sets these people apart in your judgment? How has it affected you when someone you thought had integrity has let you down?

The writer of Job sets the stage in the prologue (chs.1-2) for everything he seems to intend to teach. The primary issue addressed is that of *integrity*, so that theme is immediately introduced, defined, and applied to Job:

> **Job 1:1**
> **1** There was a man in the country of Uz named Job. He was a man of complete integrity, who feared God and turned away from evil.

The word translated "complete" here is "blameless" or "pure" or "perfect" in other major English translations and carries the idea of wholeheartedness. "Integrity" (otherwise translated "upright")

Overview & Job's Integrity, Blessing & Intercession

carries the idea into interpersonal relationships. Together, the statement describes integrity of character inside and out.

In what two ways is integrity defined by the immediate context? How do both parts of the definition depend upon God?

Does the adjective "complete" surprise you? Why or why not?

So far, who is giving this assessment of Job? How much weight does his opinion carry and why?

Job's Blessing

Another important theme of this book is *blessing*, and that theme is directly connected to that of integrity. In this book's ancient setting a man's status was expressed in possessions, including his family, particularly offspring. In Hebrew literature the numbers three, seven, and 10 were significant symbols of magnification, perfection, and fullness. His status was also closely linked to the favor – or blessing – of the god(s) he served:

> **2** He had seven sons and three daughters. **3** His estate included seven thousand sheep and goats, three thousand camels, five hundred yoke of oxen, five hundred female donkeys, and a very large number of servants. Job was the greatest man among all the people of the east.

How does the writer present Job in terms of status?

What would such a resume say about Job's God, and Job's relationship to that God in terms of blessing?

5

Job: The Cry of the Righteous Sufferer

Job's Intercession

Another key theme of Job is established right away, though it is easy to forget about once the dialogue begins in chs.3f. *Intercession* is introduced first as something Job *does*, then later as something he *needs* and *desires* and hopefully *expects* that God will provide:

> **4** His sons used to take turns having banquets at their homes. They would send an invitation to their three sisters to eat and drink with them. **5** Whenever a round of banqueting was over, Job would send for his children and purify them, rising early in the morning to offer burnt offerings for all of them. For Job thought, "Perhaps my children have sinned, having cursed God in their hearts." This was Job's regular practice.

How does Job's "regular practice" relate to his integrity?

How does Job define sin in v.5? How important is the distinction that Job is not only concerned about outward cursing but one that is "in their hearts"? Why was he concerned about his children doing this?

How do you suppose Job's concerns relate to his blessed status? To his integrity?

How do we understand integrity, blessing, and intercession to be related for us today as followers of Jesus?

How does the gospel explain that Christ's integrity and intercession leads to blessing for us?

Lesson 2 Prologue: Job's Humiliation by Satan – Test One (Ch.1, Vv.6 - 22)

The first five verses of the Prologue already established the major themes of *integrity*, *blessing*, and *intercession* featured in this story. Other major themes are introduced now, especially that of *God's sovereign rule* expressed not only in blessing but also in *humiliation* and *suffering* instigated by Job's *opponent*, Satan.

Here begins the irony. The layer of the known earthly world is peeled back to expose the heavenly spiritual realm, but only for the reader and not for Job. Only the reader learns of the cosmic challenge that will bring calamity upon Job.

God's Sovereign Rule, the Council and the Opponent

> **Job 1:6-7**
> **6** One day the sons of God came to present themselves before the Lord, and Satan also came with them. **7** The Lord asked Satan, "Where have you come from?"
>
> "From roaming through the earth," Satan answered him, "and walking around on it."

There is much going on here, but the stark reality is that of *God's absolute sovereignty*. It is apparent in part by nature of the fact that the "sons of God" are accountable to him, that they must "present themselves" to him. This phrase almost certainly refers to what is commonly called the "divine council," a group of heavenly beings who, although super-human, are mere creatures who are completely subject to God's ultimate and singular power and authority.

The fact that Satan comes with these sons of God, but that he alone is questioned, presents him as an outsider in this council. He has access, but he has been expelled to the human realm, where he "roams through the earth" and "walks around on it." "Roaming" foreshadows the unclean spirits of Mt 12:43 and Satan's own nefarious activity mentioned in 1 Pt 5:8. The term "Satan" occurs here with an article and not really as a proper name, and so simply means "the adversary." It is from the greater biblical witness that we identify him as the particular individual opponent we all think of as the Devil or the Serpent. Here he pales in comparison to the sovereign God, and he doesn't even appear after ch.2.

The Challenge

> **8** Then the LORD said to Satan, "Have you considered my servant Job? No one else on earth is like him, a man of perfect integrity, who fears God and turns away from evil."

Job: The Cry of the Righteous Sufferer

9 Satan answered the Lord, "Does Job fear God for nothing? **10** Haven't you placed a hedge around him, his household, and everything he owns? You have blessed the work of his hands, and his possessions have increased in the land. **11** But stretch out your hand and strike everything he owns, and he will surely curse you to your face."

12 "Very well," the Lord told Satan, "everything he owns is in your power. However, do not lay a hand on Job himself." So Satan left the Lord's presence.

God's sovereignty dominates the narrative. He is all-wise, speaking from his heavenly perspective, while Satan speaks from an earthly one. God is the one who brings up Job, not Satan. And God is all-powerful. Even once Satan responds with a challenge to test God's assessment, he cannot do anything unless God grants permission.

Satan uses the term "hedge" the way we often do, as a *positive* thing (like "hedge of protection"). Later in 3:23 Job will use this term in a *negative* sense, that God has "hedged him in" (trapped him). Satan's indictment is essentially this: that God is a respecter of persons who does not judge the cosmos fairly. Satan focuses on the fact that humans in their fickleness are undeserving of blessing while completely ignoring God's divine prerogative to freely and generously give blessing as he chooses. He cannot truly hope to convict the Creator, so he goes after the creature. Like a mad scientist he requests a grant to conduct experiments in the lab of suffering.

How does God's assessment of Job in v.8 compare to the writer's assessment in v.1? How striking is that assessment coming from God himself?

How does God define integrity?

How does Satan's accusation relate to the way humans account for status (vv.2-3)?

According to v.11, whose hand will bring the trouble to Job? Whose hand in v.12? How does this inform the way we think when bad things happen to us?

Job's Humiliation by Satan: Test One

How important is it to you to know that Satan can't do anything without God's permission?

Test One: Everything He Owns

Satan can do nothing without permission, but when he has it, he can be very powerful indeed! Given freedom regarding all but Job's own person, he now attacks Job by stirring up human violence and natural disasters and even supernatural ones!

> **13** One day when Job's sons and daughters were eating and drinking wine in their oldest brother's house, **14** a messenger came to Job and reported, "While the oxen were plowing and the donkeys grazing nearby, **15** the Sabeans swooped down and took them away. They struck down the servants with the sword, and I alone have escaped to tell you!"
>
> **16** He was still speaking when another messenger came and reported, "God's fire fell from heaven. It burned the sheep and the servants and devoured them, and I alone have escaped to tell you!"
>
> **17** That messenger was still speaking when yet another came and reported, "The Chaldeans formed three bands, made a raid on the camels, and took them away. They struck down the servants with the sword, and I alone have escaped to tell you!"
>
> **18** He was still speaking when another messenger came and reported, "Your sons and daughters were eating and drinking wine in their oldest brother's house. **19** Suddenly a powerful wind swept in from the desert and struck the four corners of the house. It collapsed on the young people so that they died, and I alone have escaped to tell you!"

What human agency does Satan use to attack Job? What "natural disaster"? Which attack is characterized as a supernatural event?

Test One has been carried out, and the lab is a disaster zone. Satan the Mad Scientist eagerly prepares to record the results to confirm his hypothesis that Job's true nature will blow up in toxic waste. Is his theory correct? How will this "man of complete integrity" respond? Will Job turn his back on God?

Job: The Cry of the Righteous Sufferer

The Results

> **20** Then Job stood up, tore his robe, and shaved his head. He fell to the ground and worshiped, **21** saying:
>
> Naked I came from my mother's womb,
> and naked I will leave this life.
> The LORD gives, and the LORD takes away.
> Blessed be the name of the LORD.
>
> **22** Throughout all this Job did not sin or blame God for anything.

The results must be stunning to the Scientist. This is not at all the outcome he expected, nor the one he desired! He would prefer to *falsify* the results, but our narrator faithfully reports the surprising results of Test One. At least three things are worth noting in Job's response as we consider how the themes of the prologue are beginning to unfold in the narrative:

First, Job's response is truly *human*. He is not some pious superstar who unaffectedly rises above all his circumstances. He is devastated. He immediately expresses his mourning in the manner typical for the ancient Eastern world. His heart is torn with his robe, and his pride falls to the ground with every lock of hair. He collapses in humility.

Second, what is stunning about Job's reaction is that it is *worshipful*. In lament poetry he acknowledges his poverty before the LORD. He does not *blame* God, but actually *blesses* his name. His confession is lifted specifically using the term "Yahweh," the name given (presumably later) to Moses in preparation for the Exodus. This is remarkable since we would not expect a non-Hebrew from the patriarchal period to know God by this name. Regardless, the meaning of the name, "the One Who IS," shows the confession of Job as directed to the absolutely sovereign God of creation from whom all blessings flow.

Third, Job is shown to have thus far retained his *integrity*. God's assessment is vindicated, for Job does not turn and curse God as Satan predicted. That Job's integrity is intact is expressed in two ways: 1) he "did not sin" and 2) he "did not blame God for anything." Take careful note of how Job speaks of the power behind his disasters as things continue to unfold. For now, he does not blame God for anything.

In your own times of disaster, have you blamed God or at least been tempted to do so? Have you ever questioned him or been angry with him?

Job's Humiliation by Satan: Test One

If you were in Job's sandals, how do you think you would respond to his terrible day of loss?

How has God associated his own integrity with Job's? What then is at risk in these experiments? What is NOT at risk?

How do your responses to your own tests impact God's reputation?

Lesson 3 Prologue: Job's Humiliation by Satan – Test Two (Ch.2)

We saw that the results of Test One were favorable for Job and reflected well upon God. Satan's prediction was refuted with the two-fold proclamation that Job did NOT A) sin or B) blame God for any of this calamity that befell him. So, Job's integrity was vindicated, and by extension, God's was vindicated too.

The Mad Scientist is not satisfied. His adversarial nature craves the destruction of mankind that God has made to carry his own image. He doubles down, as we get a replay of ch.1's heavenly scene. Most everything is the same, but with some tweaks, as the Scientist seeks a grant for a new experiment that will change the variables.

God's (Still) Sovereign Rule, the Council and the Opponent (Again)

> **Job 2:1-3**
> **1** One day the sons of God came again to present themselves before the Lord, and Satan also came with them to present himself before the Lord. **2** The Lord asked Satan, "Where have you come from?"
>
> "From roaming through the earth," Satan answered him, "and walking around on it."
>
> **3** Then the LORD said to Satan, "Have you considered my servant Job? No one else on earth is like him, a man of perfect integrity, who fears God and turns away from evil. He still retains his integrity, even though you incited me against him, to destroy him for no good reason."

As with any good experiment, most things are kept constant so that the impact of the variables can be discerned. The lab is set up the same. God is still sovereign, there is still accountability, and there is still an opponent who challenges the status quo. Once again, the heavenly council convenes, and once again the sons of God present themselves before the One Who Is. The intrusion of the outsider is also repeated, as the opponent, Satan, inserts himself into the scene. God singles him out, as before, with his question, "Where have you come from?" The answer is the same. Satan has been roaming the only place left for him as an outsider, as a rebel: the earth. Once again, it is God who brings up Job. His assessment too is the same, but with a minor tweak. God acknowledges the passing of Test One, which magnifies Job's integrity: he STILL retains it.

Compare the last sentence of v.3 here with 1:11-12 below:

Job: The Cry of the Righteous Sufferer

Job 1:11–12
11 But stretch out your hand and strike everything he owns, and he will surely curse you to your face."

12 "Very well," the LORD told Satan, "everything he owns is in your power. However, do not lay a hand on Job himself." So Satan left the LORD's presence.

Though Satan incited God against Job, from whose hand does it seem Job's calamity has come?

How does the phrase in 2:3, "for no good reason," relate to God's assessment of Job's integrity?

The Second Challenge

Job 2:4–6
4 "Skin for skin!" Satan answered the LORD. "A man will give up everything he owns in exchange for his life. **5** But stretch out your hand and strike his flesh and bones, and he will surely curse you to your face."

6 "Very well," the Lord told Satan, "he is in your power; only spare his life."

Once again, Satan attacks Job's integrity as a way to attack God's. The Mad Scientist's hypothesis is the same accusation as before: Job's loyalty is conditional. He tweaks his former theory – that this loyalty was based on *possessions* – to now claim that Job's loyalty is based on something more fundamental: his *physical well-being*.

As before, the accusation about Job is a red herring. Satan's real indictment is against God. The Scientist is SURE he can prove his hypothesis that God is an unjust ruler. He thinks that if he can go after Job's own body, he can finally get him to curse God. That would prove that God's blessing of Job has been undeserved. Therefore, God is a respecter of persons and biased in his rule.

As before, the Scientist seems to be blind to another possibility. What if God's blessings ARE conditional but the conditions for his blessing are not what Satan charges? What if God's blessings are not based on man's *fidelity* but rather on God's *generosity*? This would allow that there IS a natural correlation between blessedness and faithfulness. A blessed creature should naturally be

Job's Humiliation by Satan: Test Two

a thankful, faithful, and worshipful one. But it would also allow that God's choosing to bless a creature would be logically *prior to* and NOT *contingent upon* that appropriate response.

Satan's Theology

Put simply, Satan has bad theology. He apparently believes (or at least *wants* it to be true) that *man* is in the driver's seat. His premise is that God is wrong to bless his creature unless his creature proves to be *deserving* of blessing. That means the creature determines his own blessedness. If he remains true, God must bless. If he turns on God and curses him – regardless of the circumstances – then he is proven undeserving, and in Satan's view that means God *must* remove his blessing.

Notice that Satan's experiment has not only Job in mind, though he is the direct target. Satan's categorical reference in v.4 to what "a man" will do makes it clear that he is treating *this* man as a representative of *all* mankind. In this, Satan's theology agrees with the Apostle Paul's:

> **Romans 5:17–19**
> **17** If by the one man's trespass, death reigned through that one man, how much more will those who receive the overflow of grace and the gift of righteousness reign in life through the one man, Jesus Christ.
>
> **18** So then, as through one trespass there is condemnation for everyone, so also through one righteous act there is justification leading to life for everyone. **19** For just as through one man's disobedience the many were made sinners, so also through the one man's obedience the many will be made righteous.

Paul agrees that mankind has a representative that falls short. It wasn't Job in the first place, but rather Adam. Satan knows. He was there. He has utterly despised humanity from the beginning. That's why he relished his role in man's undoing, and it's why he wants to rip Job apart now.

But Satan refuses to acknowledge mankind's *other* representative mentioned by Paul. It hadn't yet played out in human history in Job's day (though it has always been accomplished even before the foundation of the world), but Jesus would be sent as that perfectly righteous and faithful representative mankind needed. Job seemed to glimpse it, and he will prove in his story to be a type of the Christ yet to come.

The Bible gives no indication that angels have such a representative, nor a redeemer. It seems their choices whether to obey God or to rebel were the one-and-done type. Satan has no one to mediate for him. He has experienced God's near presence and shunned it (Lk 10:18; 1 Jn 3:8; See also Is 14:12-15).

From what the Bible reveals, why does Satan hate mankind (including you and me) so much?

Job: The Cry of the Righteous Sufferer

Despite the vehement hatred of the Accuser, the Mad Scientist, God is still entirely in control. He has allowed Satan to initiate his attack once, and the experiment failed. Now he will allow the second attack, and this one will be a most personal assault on the righteous man. Still, even this attack is limited: "He is in your power; only spare his life."

One more time, let's take note. God is in control, but *who is bringing evil upon Job?*

Test Two: All but His Life

> **Job 2:7–9**
> **7** So Satan left the LORD's presence and infected Job with terrible boils from the soles of his feet to the top of his head. **8** Then Job took a piece of broken pottery to scrape himself while he sat among the ashes.
>
> **9** His wife said to him, "Are you still holding on to your integrity? Curse God and die!"

A short description here is sufficient for us to realize that Job's suffering is intense. Those who have had *one* boil give testimony to the fact that Job's full-body infection would have been miserable, approaching intolerable. Many of us have had some temporary malady that we have found nearly overwhelming for a while, but those who suffer with chronic illness or pain would best understand the great challenge this attack brought against Job's integrity.

We might imagine the Mad Scientist is full of glee, expecting at any moment for his experiment to yield his desired outcome. Surely, enough is enough. Job must be ready to cave at any moment. As it was with the locks of his hair, so now with every flake of decayed flesh what is left of his pride falls to the ground. Surely his resolve is soon to follow!

If his personal and physical suffering were not overwhelming enough, add to that the complete loss of emotional support from the one closest to him. We may hear echoes of Satan's own voice in that of Job's wife: *Are you kidding me?* "Curse God and die!" Perhaps Job's concerns about his children's potential for cursing would have been appropriate for his wife as well. Still, her response is understandable. Just as we pointed out in Test One with Job, so now his wife is having a natural human reaction to suffering.

Job's wife was not the subject of the experiment, though. Notice that she does use the same term the narrator and God himself have used to describe Job's character: having *integrity*. Does he still? Satan's charges depend upon Job's response. What are the results of Job's response to this second test?

Job's Humiliation by Satan: Test Two

The Results

> **10** "You speak as a foolish woman speaks," he told her. "Should we accept only good from God and not adversity?" Throughout all this Job did not sin in what he said.

We must look carefully at this outcome. First, we see that in rebuking his wife, Job positions himself as taking a different perspective. They are not experiencing different *circumstances* (except that JOB is the one with the boils), but they are choosing different *reactions* to those circumstances. Both have recently lost EVERYTHING - wealth, stuff and kids.

How have you observed that people respond differently to suffering? Specifically, have you seen others blame God for bad things that have happened, or have you done so yourself?

How does Job acknowledge God's sovereignty in saying that we "accept" both good and adversity from God?

In Job's response to the first test, he was 1) truly human, 2) worshipful, and 3) consistent in maintaining integrity. He "did not sin or blame God for anything."

How is Job's response to this second test different?

The results seem a little mixed this time. It does seem the Mad Scientist has once again been let down, failing to get his subject to curse God. However, there are hints that Job's steadfastness is beginning to waver, at least emotionally. Before, he did not *blame* God, but now he characterizes this adversity as being *from* God. Before, he mourned his losses and then *worshiped* God, but now he merely resigns himself to *accept* what God deals out. Before, it was said he "did not sin." This time the assessment is qualified. The focus seems to be on *speech*. Job rebukes his wife for her (foolish) speech, and then the narrator records that Job did not sin "in what he said." It seems that Job is really struggling now, maintaining an outward integrity but perhaps faltering inwardly.

Since Job's wife seems overcome with grief and unable to lend support, perhaps what he really needs is the comfort of a few friends. He could really use some guys who know and love him to

Job: The Cry of the Righteous Sufferer

show up and help him get through this. As the song says, "I'll get by with a little help from my friends." Right?

Job's Three Friends

> **11** Now when Job's three friends—Eliphaz the Temanite, Bildad the Shuhite, and Zophar the Naamathite—heard about all this adversity that had happened to him, each of them came from his home. They met together to go and sympathize with him and comfort him. **12** When they looked from a distance, they could barely recognize him. They wept aloud, and each man tore his robe and threw dust into the air and on his head. **13** Then they sat on the ground with him seven days and nights, but no one spoke a word to him because they saw that his suffering was very intense.

For one whole week these guys gave Job exactly what he needed: quiet sympathy. That'll preach. Unfortunately, as the story continues in the coming chapters, we'll find that these same friends screw up a good thing by opening their mouths. That'll preach too. For now, let's glean a little more about the situation as they find it, and then we'll reflect a little bit on the whole affair.

We can't know a whole lot about these friends, but here is a brief survey of what seems available to us. Like Job, these guys do not appear to be Hebrew. (They may well be contemporary with Abram or predate God's covenant with him.) They seemed to have traveled quite a bit to come to Job, apparently from different regions or countries. Their purpose is clearly stated: they "met together to go and sympathize with [Job] and comfort him." Upon arrival, they took up typical actions of mourning, much like Job did in ch.1. The seven-day period of silence seems to also have been a cultural norm for corporate mourning.

Eliphaz bears the name given to one of Esau's sons (Gn 36:4), but almost certainly cannot be that Eliphaz. There is a descendant of that Eliphaz named Teman (v.14), which may hint at a Temanite people group connected to Job's Eliphaz. However, the strongest possible link for Eliphaz is that he is apparently *from* Teman, a city in ancient Edom that was known for wisdom (Jr 49:7). He certainly will speak as though he carries such a reputation as a wise man! Bildad is even more obscure. Some speculate that as a Shuhite he may be descended from Shua, one of the sons of Abraham and Keturah (Gn 25:2). However, this cannot be confirmed. Zophar is a name not used elsewhere in Scripture, and apart from Gn 4:22 there are no prospects to even identify a clan of Naamathites. These obscurities related to Job's friends simply inform us that who they are is not important to understanding their contributions in this story. It is enough to know that they (along with Job) represent the traditions and wisdom of the ancient east.

Job's Humiliation by Satan: Test Two

How do these verses affirm Job was "the greatest man among all the people of the east" (1:3)?

What terms here speak to the obvious degree of Job's suffering? (Compare v.12a with Is 52:14)

Reflection

How would you assess the results regarding Job? Is he vindicated as still retaining his integrity? Has Satan gotten him to curse God?

How does this outcome seem to reflect upon God? Does it feel dangerous for God to hang his reputation on the response of one human?

Paul, in 1 Corinthians 10:13 says, "God is faithful; he will not allow you to be tempted beyond what you are able, but with the temptation he will also provide the way out so that you may be able to bear it."

How does this inform our perspective of what God allows in this testing of Job?

Lesson 4 Dialogue: Job's Lament (Ch.3)

As we already saw, we know from 2:13 that Job's friends sit with him for seven days saying nothing. It seems that silence characterizes that whole mourning period, because ch.3 opens with a transitionary statement: "After this, Job began to speak and cursed the day he was born."

Now, the writer of this book could have simply written that statement and moved on. We know that up to this point it was recorded, "Job did not sin in what he said" (2:10). In fact, he reproved his wife for speaking foolishly. It is possible, perhaps even likely, that Job was himself struggling so much internally that he – as we say – "held his tongue" so that he would not defame God publicly. If so, that would be a mighty struggle, to spend seven days biting one's tongue.

Job's Restraint

Even when the dam breaks, we still find Job remarkable in his restraint. He *does* begin to curse, but it is not *God* he curses – unless you argue that he does so indirectly. No, he curses a *day* – the day he was born.

Rather than simply recording propositional statements like that of the first verse here, the writer draws us *into* Job's suffering. With dramatic, sometimes over-the-top poetry, we feel every stab of pain with Job. All these centuries later we are able to commiserate with Job a little bit like his three friends did. What could they say? What could we? We endure through verse after verse to realize, once again, Job's utter humanity. He is like us. He believes what he believes about God. He knows God to a point. But this is not making sense. So, he cries out. Perhaps with his last shred of integrity, the best he can muster is to redirect his pain and anger at some THING instead of at the God he is convinced could have prevented all this.

Let's enter into Job's suffering as we read his lament:

Job's Lament

> **Job 3:2–26**
> **2** He said:
>
> > **3** May the day I was born perish,
> > and the night that said,
> > "A boy is conceived."

Job: The Cry of the Righteous Sufferer

4 If only that day had turned to darkness!
May God above not care about it,
or light shine on it.
5 May darkness and gloom reclaim it,
and a cloud settle over it.
May what darkens the day terrify it.
6 If only darkness had taken that night away!
May it not appear among the days of the year
or be listed in the calendar.
7 Yes, may that night be barren;
may no joyful shout be heard in it.
8 Let those who curse days
condemn it,
those who are ready to rouse Leviathan.
9 May its morning stars grow dark.
May it wait for daylight but have none;
may it not see the breaking of dawn.
10 For that night did not shut
the doors of my mother's womb,
and hide sorrow from my eyes.

11 Why was I not stillborn;
why didn't I die as I came from the womb?
12 Why did the knees receive me,
and why were there breasts for me to nurse?
13 Now I would certainly be lying down in peace;
I would be asleep.
Then I would be at rest
14 with the kings and counselors of the earth,
who rebuilt ruined cities for themselves,
15 or with princes who had gold,
who filled their houses with silver.
16 Or why was I not hidden like a miscarried child,
like infants who never see daylight?
17 There the wicked cease to make trouble,
and there the weary find rest.
18 The captives are completely at rest;
they do not hear a taskmaster's voice.
19 Both small and great are there,
and the slave is set free from his master.

Job's Lament

20 Why is light given to one burdened with grief,
and life to those whose existence is bitter,
21 who wait for death, but it does not come,
and search for it more than for hidden treasure,
22 who are filled with much joy
and are glad when they reach the grave?
23 Why is life given to a man whose path is hidden,
whom God has hedged in?
24 I sigh when food is put before me,
and my groans pour out like water.
25 For the thing I feared has overtaken me,
and what I dreaded has happened to me.
26 I cannot relax or be calm;
I have no rest, for turmoil has come.

Wow! What anguish! Let's examine this lament further in three sections.

Cursing His Day
First, Job targets the day of his birth in vv.3-10. Since the day did in fact happen, he wishes it could now be erased, forgotten or blotted out. He presents it as a thing brought out of darkness, and he wishes that darkness would reclaim it (v.5). Even though he acknowledges that it contained at least the potential for joy (v.7), he now would prefer that it be stricken from the calendar, as though it never existed.

Notice here that for God to "care about" this day or to "shine a light on it" is characterized as a *bad* thing. Similarly, in other OT literature it can be either a good thing or a bad thing to be seen by or remembered by God. Here, and at this point in his life, Job clearly sees it as bad.

What words or phrases in vv.3-10 describe Job's anguish?

Has there ever been a day you have wished you could "remove from the calendar"? Why?

Notice the phrase "rouse Leviathan" in v.8. That creature will be mentioned four times by God in ch.41. It is an immensely powerful sea creature (think dragon or maybe Godzilla) that represents the (potentially evil) power of chaos. Job invites those who want to stir up THAT kind of trouble to curse the day of his own birth. Yikes! Job explains why he wishes someone could blot out the day of his birth: "For that night did not shut the doors of my mother's womb." As a result, it did not "hide sorrow from my eyes."

Cursing His Birth

Since he cannot *erase* the day of his birth, in v.10 Job shifts from cursing the *day* of his birth to cursing his *birth* itself. Throughout this section from vv.11-19, Job emphasizes that the tragedy of death would have been preferable to the grief he suffers now. He uses the parallel terms of "stillborn" and "miscarried" to paint a delayed death wish. Whatever joy he has experienced in life has been so entirely swallowed up in grief that he would prefer to have never had joy than to have lost it like this. He paints shriveling up in starvation (v.12) as superior to his current state, for at least in death he would be "at rest" (v.13).

In fact, Job makes a big deal of resting in this section. Consistent with other wisdom poetry, Job describes the grave or the afterlife as the great equalizer. In death, all types of people receive peace and rest, whether kings or counselors or princes (vv.14-15), whether master or slave, small or great (vv.18-19). Notice though, that the wicked do *not* make the list of those resting, but rather that death is a place where *others* rest from the *troubling* of the wicked (v.17).

Job is venting his pain, and not drafting a careful theology about the afterlife. Still, we get a glimpse into his ancient mindset about such things.

To what extent is it true that death MAY bring rest and peace?

Consider what the writer of Hebrews tells us about rest. He cited the OT example of the Israelites who wandered in the wilderness because of their rebellion against God. About them, he writes:

> **Hebrews 3:7–11 (CSB)**
> **7** Therefore, as the Holy Spirit says:
>
>> Today, if you hear his voice,
>> **8** do not harden your hearts as in the rebellion,
>> on the day of testing in the wilderness,
>> **9** where your ancestors tested me, tried me,
>> and saw my works **10** for forty years.
>> Therefore I was provoked to anger with that generation
>> and said, "They always go astray in their hearts,
>> and they have not known my ways."

Job's Lament

> **11** So I swore in my anger,
> "They will not enter my rest."

Those who rebelled found no rest, but rest *was* available. He goes on to say, "we who have believed (DO) enter the rest" (4:3, supplement mine).

How does Job's craving for rest and peace point forward to the gospel truths we understand about those things we have in Christ?

Job is certainly finding no physical or emotional rest right now. In fact, he seems to even be *spiritually* distressed. We already saw that Satan had flawed theology. In the coming chapters we'll see that Job is wrestling with aspects of his *own* theology that just don't seem to jibe with what he is experiencing.

Questioning and the "Thing" Job Fears

Job is questioning. He has already begun a series of "why" questions in the second section of his lament (4x in vv.11-12; then in vv.12 and 16). "Why didn't I die in the womb, or upon birth?" Now he asks two more: "Why was I given light?" (v.20) and "Why was I given life?" (v.23). Everything is upside down. Light only exposes grief and bitterness. Death, however, is a treasure that brings joy and gladness (vv.21-22), while ordinary means of sustenance (food) only bring a sigh (v.24).

Despite his groaning, of course Job realizes he can't alter the calendar and erase the day of his birth. He also cannot change his own history by erasing his birth from that day. My wife and I have developed a sort of shorthand word for moments like this: "iiwii" (pronounced "ee - wee"). It is an acronym for "It is what it is." Job concludes his lament with a gloomy description of his current situation. With two couplets the writer lets us peer a bit into not only Job's distressed state but also his theology. Here they are again:

> **25** For the thing I feared has overtaken me,
> and what I dreaded has happened to me.
> **26** I cannot relax or be calm;
> I have no rest, for turmoil has come.

The parallel terms of "thing I feared" and "what I dreaded" describe a situation that had been a potentiality for Job. No more. Now it is actuality, for it "has overtaken me" and "happened to me."

What do you think is this "thing" that Job has dreaded and that has now happened?

Job: The Cry of the Righteous Sufferer

When we seek to understand to what "thing" Job is referring, the most obvious context is his catastrophic situation. It seems reasonable to think Job has dreaded the loss of his greatness in all its expressions. The OT wisdom of Solomon tells us that with riches come much worry (Ecc 5:12-13). The NT wisdom of James says the same (Jas 5:1-2). Perhaps Job is struggling to do what James commands: "Let the rich boast in his humiliation because he will pass away like a flower of the field" (1:10). Remember Job's ancient contextual views, the strong association between allegiance to a deity and the blessings of material and familial wealth. Was Job fearing the loss of his great status and comfort?

Given the descriptions of Job's integrity in the prologue, we have good reason to believe that the "thing" Job fears goes deeper. It seems likely that Job is genuinely concerned that he (or previously, also his children) might offend God. He seems to be a man that would be bothered by that, regardless of the impact to his social status. This would prompt such a rebuke of his wife as we saw in 2:10.

Perhaps our understanding of Job's "thing" which he dreaded should include a sense of disconnectedness from God. God's people often describe times when it feels he is far off, whether it seems they have done something to cause it or not. As we read on, this feeling is implied in Job's language, for he asks more than once for God to show up. (God does.)

For now, let's consider Job's last couplet explaining his frustrated state. He "cannot relax or be calm." Once again, he says he has "no rest."

What does Job give as the reason that he has no rest?

How can circumstances dictate whether WE feel like we can or cannot rest?

Job's Lament

Reflection

How might our own lamenting in difficult times be healthy (spiritually, physically, emotionally, etc.)? How might lament be or become <u>unhealthy</u>?

Why is it important for us to hear and believe the gospel in those times?

Lesson 5 Dialogue: Round One: Eliphaz V. Job (Chs.4 - 7)

Job has been decimated. His emotional distress and spiritual confusion are completely understandable, especially given his physical malady on top of everything else. His suffering is total, impacting his whole person. He has cried out in his frustration, cursing the day of his birth, his birth event itself, and his present existence. Now, his friends also break their silence.

Eliphaz's Rebuke

Eliphaz is first. He acknowledges Job's exhaustion:

> **Job 4:1–2 (CSB)**
> **1** Then Eliphaz the Temanite replied:
>
> **2** Should anyone try to speak with you
> when you are exhausted?
> Yet who can keep from speaking?

The Friend's Limited Perspective

To say Job's reaction is understandable is to speak from the perspective we have as readers, but this is not so much the perspective of Job's friends. Remember the irony that is so key to this story. Job doesn't know all that we do, but he *does* know that he did not bring this calamity upon himself by any sinful action or collapse of integrity. In fact, even under this great pressure he restrains himself from cursing God for his circumstances, choosing to curse himself instead. Job's friends *cannot* know Job's innocence, and so do not see Job as restrained but more like a loose cannon.

The friends may understand Job's reaction to a point, but when he finally opens his mouth to lament and curse himself, it is too much. Why would Job's reaction be intolerable to Eliphaz, so much so that he cannot "keep from speaking"? It must be because he is convinced that Job's verbal lament is somehow inappropriate. Why is that? It seems Eliphaz is convinced that Job must be aware that this calamity IS somehow his own doing. In a moment, we'll explore why he would draw that conclusion.

Why is it important for us when entering a friend's suffering to realize our own limited perspective?

Job: The Cry of the Righteous Sufferer

Retribution Theology
The context of the book reveals that these men (Job included) have to this point shared the same theology, what is often called Retribution Theology. It says, "Live rightly and God will bless you." This is true to a point, but not true enough. This belief system also rigidly holds related conclusions that *may* be true but are not *necessarily* true. These related statements put man in the driver's seat but ignore his imperfections of both action and heart. To that first law above they add, "Screw up and God must *not* bless you," making Satan's error of ignoring or disallowing God's divine prerogative to be generous, to freely give grace even to the one who is not true to him.

One corollary of Retribution Theology is especially relevant to Job's story, the purpose of this book, and much of what Job's friends will argue. It says, "If things are going badly, then you *must* have screwed up, and God is hammering you for it." Another way to put it is, "When things go wrong you must be getting what you *deserve*. You must have *sinned*." This explains Eliphaz's quick turn from quiet sympathy to harsh rebuke. His Retribution Theology does not allow any other explanation for Job's situation than Job's own sin. God is perfectly just, so Job must be at fault.

Retribution Theology is behind that question the disciples asked Jesus in Jn 9:1-2 upon seeing the blind man: "Who sinned, this man or his parents, that he was born blind?" The corrective Jesus gave his students could effectively summarize the whole of Job: "Neither this man nor his parents sinned. This came about *so that God's works might be displayed in him*" (italics mine). Retribution Theology cannot be a suitable theology because it does not account for all possibilities, nor for God's heavenly purposes and his loving generosity.

It is worth noting once again how much Retribution Theology resembles today's Prosperity Theology, which says, "If life is not what you want it to be right now, it must be because you do not have enough faith. If you truly have enough faith, you can have your best life now." In this case the "sin" is one of not having enough faith.

From Sympathy to Judgment
Despite its inadequacies, it becomes more and more apparent that Retribution Theology is indeed the perspective of Job's friends. Eliphaz cannot hold back. His brief acknowledgement of Job's exhaustion quickly begins to feel like a mere concession to half-heartedly excuse Job's crazy talk. He must rebuke Job for what he thinks is an offense against God's character, for if Job did not cause this by sinning, then – under Retribution Theology – God must be unjust. That cannot be true.

> **3** Indeed, you have instructed many
> and have strengthened weak hands.
> **4** Your words have steadied the one who was stumbling
> and braced the knees that were buckling.

Round One: Eliphaz V. Job

5 But now that this has happened to you,
you have become exhausted.
It strikes you, and you are dismayed.
6 Isn't your piety your confidence,
and the integrity of your life your hope?
7 Consider: Who has perished when he was innocent?
Where have the honest been destroyed?
8 In my experience, those who plow injustice
and those who sow trouble reap the same.
9 They perish at a single blast from God
and come to an end by the breath of his nostrils.
10 The lion may roar and the fierce lion growl,
but the teeth of young lions are broken.
11 The strong lion dies if it catches no prey,
and the cubs of the lioness are scattered.

How does Eliphaz – even in his rebuke – affirm Job's reputation for being upright and righteous?

What is ironic about the phrase, "in my experience" in v.8, and how does that tie to our first observation about his limited perspective?

When have YOU judged things wrongly due to your limited knowledge?

What is Eliphaz already beginning to imply in v.7?

How does the Law of Sowing and Reaping (v.8) relate to Retribution Theology?

Job: The Cry of the Righteous Sufferer

Eliphaz cranks up the poetic rhetoric even more dramatically:

> **12** A word was brought to me in secret;
> my ears caught a whisper of it.
> **13** Among unsettling thoughts from visions in the night,
> when deep sleep comes over men,
> **14** fear and trembling came over me
> and made all my bones shake.
> **15** I felt a draft on my face,
> and the hair on my body stood up.
> **16** A figure stood there,
> but I could not recognize its appearance;
> a form loomed before my eyes.
> I heard a whispering voice:
> **17** "Can a mortal be righteous before God?
> Can a man be more pure than his Maker?"
> **18** If God puts no trust in his servants
> and he charges his angels with foolishness,
> **19** how much more those who dwell in clay houses,
> whose foundation is in the dust,
> who are crushed like a moth!
> **20** They are smashed to pieces from dawn to dusk;
> they perish forever while no one notices.
> **21** Are their tent cords not pulled up?
> They die without wisdom.

Who is Eliphaz talking about in v.19, and what are the "clay houses"?

What seems to be the point made by this Watcher's statement in v.17 (compare 7:17-20) and then Eliphaz's interpretation that follows in vv.18-21?

Eliphaz really pulls off the gloves now:

Round One: Eliphaz V. Job

Job 5:1

> **1** Call out! Will anyone answer you?
> Which of the holy ones will you turn to?
> **2** For anger kills a fool,
> and jealousy slays the gullible.
> **3** I have seen a fool taking root,
> but I immediately pronounced a curse on his home.
> **4** His children are far from safety.
> They are crushed at the city gate,
> with no one to rescue them.
> **5** The hungry consume his harvest,
> even taking it out of the thorns.
> The thirsty pant for his children's wealth.
> **6** For distress does not grow out of the soil,
> and trouble does not sprout from the ground.
> **7** But humans are born for trouble
> as surely as sparks fly upward.

Hear the sarcasm in v.1! In reply to Job's lament, Eliphaz essentially says, "Cry all you want. That won't fix this. And the holy ones (heavenly beings) won't help you either." Hear the condemnation in his words in v.3, essentially calling Job a fool that deserves cursing! (That's ironic, because Job just cursed himself, and now while Eliphaz rebukes him for it he says he deserves cursing for acting like this proverbial "fool.") Can you believe the insensitivity? Job just lost all his children in one day. Now, mere weeks later, Eliphaz looks down his snout and says, "His children are far from safety." He is all but implying that Job is responsible for the death of his children!

How have you seen rigid and inadequate worldviews like Retribution Theology foster judgmentalism like this?

Expert Advice

Eliphaz seems to back off the gas pedal just slightly, moving on from sarcasm to direct speech. Still, he speaks down from his lofty view to offer his advice as a seasoned expert:

> **8** However, if I were you, I would appeal to God
> and would present my case to him.
> **9** He does great and unsearchable things,
> wonders without number.

Job: The Cry of the Righteous Sufferer

10 He gives rain to the earth
and sends water to the fields.
11 He sets the lowly on high,
and mourners are lifted to safety.
12 He frustrates the schemes of the crafty
so that they achieve no success.
13 He traps the wise in their craftiness
so that the plans of the deceptive
are quickly brought to an end.
14 They encounter darkness by day,
and they grope at noon
as if it were night.
15 He saves the needy from their sharp words
and from the clutches of the powerful.
16 So the poor have hope,
and injustice shuts its mouth.
17 See how happy is the person whom God corrects;
so do not reject the discipline of the Almighty.
18 For he wounds but he also bandages;
he strikes, but his hands also heal.
19 He will rescue you from six calamities;
no harm will touch you in seven.
20 In famine he will redeem you from death,
and in battle, from the power of the sword.
21 You will be safe from slander
and not fear destruction when it comes.
22 You will laugh at destruction and hunger
and not fear the land's wild creatures.
23 For you will have a covenant with the stones of the field,
and the wild animals will be at peace with you.
24 You will know that your tent is secure,
and nothing will be missing when you inspect your home.
25 You will also know that your offspring will be many
and your descendants like the grass of the earth.
26 You will approach the grave in full vigor,
as a stack of sheaves is gathered in its season.
27 We have investigated this, and it is true!
Hear it and understand it for yourself.

Round One: Eliphaz V. Job

How does this section (esp. vv.19-26) draw from and support Retribution Theology? How does it support material wealth, health, and security as the primary (or even only) signs of blessing by God?

What do you think Eliphaz is suggesting in v.8 that Job should do when he says, "appeal to God" and "present [your] case to him"?

Though the flowery rhetoric may camouflage it somewhat for a while, Eliphaz makes his assessment plain in v.17. Why is this happening to Job? It is the Lord's discipline. Discipline for what? Job must have sinned somehow. In fact, given the severity of the calamity, he must have *really* sinned. What does Eliphaz recommend? Job should confess his sin and receive God's correction. Why? Because God "wounds, but he also bandages; he strikes, but his hands also heal" (v.18).

What does Eliphaz get <u>right</u> about God so far?

Notice once again the term "hands" here in v.18. In 1:11 and 2:4 Satan incited God to bring calamity to Job by God's own *hand*. However, in 1:12, in giving sovereign permission for Satan to attack Job, God says Job is in *Satan's* power. Then he uses a parallel statement in decreeing Satan's limits: "Do not lay a *hand* on Job himself."

Whose "hand" does Eliphaz see at work in Job's disastrous situation?

Whose "hand" does the narrator reveal is really behind it?

Job: The Cry of the Righteous Sufferer

Compare/contrast three types of troubling situations: A) sowing & reaping (natural consequences), B) God's discipline of his own (correction) and C) God's judgment of the wicked (punishment). How does this perspective of "the hand" behind the trouble differ in each case?

Job's Response

The pump has been primed. Once Job broke the silence with his lament, he began this avalanche of debate speeches. He fends off his friend's accusations, but not immediately. First, he reasserts his anguish:

His Devastation

> **Job 6:1–13**
> **1** Then Job answered:
>
> > **2** If only my grief could be weighed
> > and my devastation placed with it on the scales.
> > **3** For then it would outweigh the sand of the seas!
> > That is why my words are rash.
> > **4** Surely the arrows of the Almighty have pierced me;
> > my spirit drinks their poison.
> > God's terrors are arrayed against me.
> > **5** Does a wild donkey bray over fresh grass
> > or an ox low over its fodder?
> > **6** Is bland food eaten without salt?
> > Is there flavor in an egg white?
> > **7** I refuse to touch them;
> > they are like contaminated food.
> >
> > **8** If only my request would be granted
> > and God would provide what I hope for:
> > **9** that he would decide to crush me,
> > to unleash his power and cut me off!
> > **10** It would still bring me comfort,
> > and I would leap for joy in unrelenting pain
> > that I have not denied the words of the Holy One.

Round One: Eliphaz V. Job

> **11** What strength do I have, that I should continue to hope?
> What is my future, that I should be patient?
> **12** Is my strength that of stone,
> or my flesh made of bronze?
> **13** Since I cannot help myself,
> the hope for success has been banished from me.

Eliphaz's sympathy wore out in one sentence: "Should anyone try to speak with you when you are exhausted?" Job goes much further in reasserting his despondent state.

What words or phrases does Job use to describe himself and his horrible situation?

According to v.4, whose hand does JOB see as being the one behind his calamity? How is this correct, and how is it incorrect? How does this agree with Eliphaz, and how does it disagree?

How does this reveal Job's own Retribution Theology? How does it explain his confusion?

His Friends

Job, like Eliphaz, sees this calamity as coming from the Lord (see 2:10). He does NOT agree with why it has come. Though he can't make sense of it (in terms of his own Retribution Theology perspective), he knows he did not cause it directly by any particular sin.

Having acknowledged his situation, Job now replies to Eliphaz. Just as his friend could not restrain comment, so now Job cannot resist letting him know how he feels about his harsh treatment. His response is equally brash:

> **14** A despairing man should receive loyalty from his friends,
> even if he abandons the fear of the Almighty.
> **15** My brothers are as treacherous as a wadi,
> as seasonal streams that overflow
> **16** and become darkened because of ice,
> and the snow melts into them.

Job: The Cry of the Righteous Sufferer

> **17** The wadis evaporate in warm weather;
> they disappear from their channels in hot weather.
> **18** Caravans turn away from their routes,
> go up into the desert, and perish.
> **19** The caravans of Tema look for these streams.
> The traveling merchants of Sheba hope for them.
> **20** They are ashamed because they had been confident of finding water.
> When they arrive there, they are disappointed.
> **21** So this is what you have now become to me.
> When you see something dreadful, you are afraid.
> **22** Have I ever said, "Give me something"
> or "Pay a bribe for me from your wealth"
> **23** or "Deliver me from the enemy's hand"
> or "Redeem me from the hand of the ruthless"?

With friends like this – right? Job responds with as much vitriol as was dealt out by Eliphaz. His statement in v.14 is over the top with hyperbole, for it is doubtful Job really would find much consolation in the loyalty of true friends if he had abandoned his fear of the Almighty. Clearly, he is using such strong language to convey his sense of betrayal by Eliphaz. This is a sharp blow on top of the already confusing struggle to think *God* may have abandoned – worse, *targeted* – him for no apparent reason. Now his flesh-and-blood friends have bailed too? It's too much! Given their history (vv.22-23), Job deserved better.

How would you summarize what Job means by "this is what you have become to me" (vv.15-20)?

His Righteousness

After Job vents emotionally, he returns to the *objective* issue still at hand – his righteousness. To reassert that, he leans into a *subjective* reality. Eliphaz cannot refute Job's claim to be undeserving of this disaster, because Eliphaz can't know Job's heart.

> **24** Teach me, and I will be silent.
> Help me understand what I did wrong.
> **25** How painful honest words can be!
> But what does your rebuke prove?
> **26** Do you think that you can disprove my words
> or that a despairing man's words are mere wind?

Round One: Eliphaz V. Job

> **27** No doubt you would cast lots for a fatherless child
> and negotiate a price to sell your friend.

Harsh words from Job, but payment in kind. Eliphaz has accused Job of sin, and now Job responds with a character attack of his own. Still, the person in question is Job. He has pushed back on what Eliphaz could *not* know, that Job has not cursed God in his heart. Now, he draws back to what Eliphaz *could* know, Job's outward actions:

> **28** But now, please look at me;
> I will not lie to your face.
> **29** Reconsider; don't be unjust.
> Reconsider; my righteousness is still the issue.
> **30** Is there injustice on my tongue
> or can my palate not taste disaster?

How is the issue related to both Job's righteousness AND God's?

At some point, either here or in the next few verses, and certainly by v.12, Job shifts from addressing Eliphaz to speaking to the Lord. Job bemoans his fate:

Job 7
1 Isn't each person consigned to forced labor on earth?
Are not his days like those of a hired worker?
2 Like a slave he longs for shade;
like a hired worker he waits for his pay.
3 So I have been made to inherit months of futility,
and troubled nights have been assigned to me.
4 When I lie down I think,
"When will I get up?"
But the evening drags on endlessly,
and I toss and turn until dawn.
5 My flesh is clothed with maggots and encrusted with dirt.
My skin forms scabs and then oozes.

6 My days pass more swiftly than a weaver's shuttle;
they come to an end without hope.
7 Remember that my life is but a breath.
My eye will never again see anything good.

Job: The Cry of the Righteous Sufferer

> **8** The eye of anyone who looks on me
> will no longer see me.
> Your eyes will look for me, but I will be gone.
> **9** As a cloud fades away and vanishes,
> so the one who goes down to Sheol will never rise again.
> **10** He will never return to his house;
> his hometown will no longer remember him.

How have you seen the longing (v.2) and helplessness (v.3) that comes in suffering lead to hopelessness (v.7)?

How can longing and helplessness become a positive thing?

God's Target?
As Job goes on, it becomes even more clear that he sees this all as coming from God's hand. Remember that Job is (at least throughout the narrative of this book) unaware of the satanic challenge and experiment. Realize Job's theology does not offer an explanation for his situation. He is faced with a contradiction that Retribution Theology cannot resolve: If A) God's integrity is intact AND B) Job's integrity is also intact, then how can Job's life be swallowed up in disaster? Job is convinced both A and B are true, but here he is in the middle of suffering, all the same. His unfolding story will begin to demolish the walls of his insufficient theology and reveal the true generosity behind God's blessings, but for now, he is still processing:

> **11** Therefore I will not restrain my mouth.
> I will speak in the anguish of my spirit;
> I will complain in the bitterness of my soul.
> **12** Am I the sea or a sea monster,
> that you keep me under guard?
> **13** When I say, "My bed will comfort me,
> and my couch will ease my complaint,"
> **14** then you frighten me with dreams,
> and terrify me with visions,
> **15** so that I prefer strangling—
> death rather than life in this body.

Round One: Eliphaz V. Job

16 I give up! I will not live forever.
Leave me alone, for my days are a breath.

17 What is a mere human, that you think so highly of him
and pay so much attention to him?
18 You inspect him every morning,
and put him to the test every moment.
19 Will you ever look away from me,
or leave me alone long enough to swallow?
20 If I have sinned, what have I done to you,
Watcher of humanity?
Why have you made me your target,
so that I have become a burden to you?
21 Why not forgive my sin
and pardon my iniquity?
For soon I will lie down in the grave.
You will eagerly seek me, but I will be gone.

How does the "inspection" of v.18 relate to the sons of God "present[ing] themselves to the Lord" in 1:6 and 2:1?

In the Bible, God's attention can be a good thing or a bad thing:

Matthew 10:29–31 (CSB)
29 Aren't two sparrows sold for a penny? Yet not one of them falls to the ground without your Father's consent. **30** But even the hairs of your head have all been counted. **31** So don't be afraid; you are worth more than many sparrows.

How does God's attention and gaze (v.19 above) upon a human here contrast with the way it is presented by Jesus in Mt? How is Job's perspective in his own case wrong?

Job: The Cry of the Righteous Sufferer

Reflection on the First Exchange

Retribution Theology has driven the dialogue from the start, and irony is woven in. Both Eliphaz and Job believe bad things should not happen to righteous people, but they are drawing different conclusions about the bad things happening to Job. Both agree God cannot be to blame though both see this as God's hand (Eliphaz for correction, Job for, well, he doesn't *know* what). Eliphaz then concludes Job must be the culprit, and that means he must have sinned. Job knows that is not the case – at least he's *pretty* sure (7:20). At minimum, he defends himself as though he's convinced. But he still doesn't know what to do with all this. The lack of an explanation from Retribution Theology is perplexing to Job, and very informative to us, the readers. He knows something else MUST be going on behind the obvious. We know something else IS going on, and we even know much about what that is. We are reminded that we sometimes sit in Job's position, and we are helped by his story. We can realize that more is happening than WE know too.

Have you ever felt like God's target?

Have you ever felt like a friend's target, like they were judging you without cause?

How can Job's story help you with your own suffering, and even with your own judgmental friends?

Lesson 6 Dialogue: Round One: Bildad V. Job (Chs.8 - 10)

With Eliphaz's opening comments and his tone we already began to wonder (along with Job), "With friends like this, who needs enemies?" The dialogue does not soften as Job's next friend pipes in, for, as we shall see, his Retribution Theology paradigm drives him to also treat Job as the guilty party rather than a victim. It seems there is no room for mercy or compassion, but only cold, hard judgments and accusations. Bildad barely revs the engine before he mashes the accelerator to the mat:

Bildad's Judgment

Presumptions

Job 8:1–7
1 Then Bildad the Shuhite replied:

> **2** How long will you go on saying these things?
> Your words are a blast of wind.
> **3** Does God pervert justice?
> Does the Almighty pervert what is right?
> **4** Since your children sinned against him,
> he gave them over to their rebellion.
> **5** But if you earnestly seek God
> and ask the Almighty for mercy,
> **6** if you are pure and upright,
> then he will move even now on your behalf
> and restore the home where your righteousness dwells.
> **7** Then, even if your beginnings were modest,
> your final days will be full of prosperity.

What presumption does Bildad clearly make about God in v.3?

What presumption does he make about Job's children in v.4?

Job: The Cry of the Righteous Sufferer

What presumption does he make about Job himself in vv.5-7?

How does Bildad show his Retribution Theology in his presumptions and conclusions?

Do you see any theological errors in these verses? If so, where, and what are they?

How have you observed people making presumptions about others in distress, that they "had it coming?"

Historical Evidence

Eliphaz drew from his personal experience in making his case from Retribution Theology that Job must be at fault. Bildad throws the net more broadly to draw evidence from those who have come before, as though hearing the rebuke from "the previous generation" might soften the blow:

> **8** For ask the previous generation,
> and pay attention to what their ancestors discovered,
> **9** since we were born only yesterday and know nothing.
> Our days on earth are but a shadow.
> **10** Will they not teach you and tell you
> and speak from their understanding?
> **11** Does papyrus grow where there is no marsh?
> Do reeds flourish without water?
> **12** While still uncut shoots,
> they would dry up quicker than any other plant.
> **13** Such is the destiny of all who forget God;
> the hope of the godless will perish.
> **14** His source of confidence is fragile;
> what he trusts in is a spider's web.

Round One: Bildad V. Job

> **15** He leans on his web, but it doesn't stand firm.
> He grabs it, but it does not hold up.
> **16** He is a well-watered plant in the sunshine;
> his shoots spread out over his garden.
> **17** His roots are intertwined around a pile of rocks.
> He looks for a home among the stones.
> **18** If he is uprooted from his place,
> it will deny knowing him, saying, "I never saw you."
> **19** Surely this is the joy of his way of life;
> yet others will sprout from the dust.

What does Bildad say about those who "forget God"?

What is Bildad's implied accusation in v.13?

How are the discoveries and lessons of previous generations important and good for our theology?

What is the danger of considering a view (like Retribution Theology) as sufficient and sure for sound theology simply because it is traditional? To what must we compare such traditions to test them?

Bittersweet Prediction

> **20** Look, God does not reject a person of integrity,
> and he will not support evildoers.
> **21** He will yet fill your mouth with laughter
> and your lips with a shout of joy.

Job: The Cry of the Righteous Sufferer

> **22** Your enemies will be clothed with shame;
> the tent of the wicked will no longer exist.

Do you see anything wrong with Bildad's assertions here?

Do you see anything wrong with Bildad's <u>application</u> of these assertions?

Job's Response

The Impossible Appeal

As Job responds to his second friend, we find clues early on that Job shares Bildad's belief in the basic propositions of Retribution Theology. However, the longer Job speaks the more we see him struggle with the apparent contradictions with his own situation. He knows God cannot be unjust, but because he also believes himself to be suffering unjustly, Job begins to speak in hypothetical "if's," as though he might appeal to God:

> **Job 9:1–13**
> **1** Then Job answered:
>
> **2** Yes, I know what you've said is true,
> but how can a person be justified before God?
> **3** If one wanted to take him to court,
> he could not answer God once in a thousand times.
>
> **4** God is wise and all-powerful.
> Who has opposed him and come out unharmed?
> **5** He removes mountains without their knowledge,
> overturning them in his anger.
> **6** He shakes the earth from its place
> so that its pillars tremble.
> **7** He commands the sun not to shine
> and seals off the stars.

Round One: Bildad V. Job

> **8** He alone stretches out the heavens
> and treads on the waves of the sea.
> **9** He makes the stars: the Bear, Orion,
> the Pleiades, and the constellations of the southern sky.
> **10** He does great and unsearchable things,
> wonders without number.
> **11** If he passed by me, I wouldn't see him;
> if he went by, I wouldn't recognize him.
> **12** If he snatches something, who can stop him?
> Who can ask him, "What are you doing?"
> **13** God does not hold back his anger;
> Rahab's assistants cringe in fear beneath him!

Job argues that God is beyond appealing to because of his great power (vv.4-9), his transcendence (vv.10-11), and his divine prerogative to do whatever he wants (vv.12-13). Here Job begins to wander into what Satan misses in his own theology, that God has sovereign prerogative to give undeserved blessings, at least in this life.

Retribution Theology is right that God must be perfectly just, but it does not truly understand God as generous and patient. (Remember, with Retribution Theology the *creature* is in the driver's seat.) It sees divine free will as constrained by strict justice (retribution) but not as free in regard to generosity. This theology also holds that God must show himself as just in regard to the events of *this age*. It does not acknowledge that God may allow apparent injustice in this age for his divine purposes so long as he brings those things to justice in the *age to come*.

How may a rebel who rejects God get treated "unjustly" by getting BETTER than she deserves?

How may a suffering believer get treated "unjustly" by getting WORSE than she deserves?

How will the age to come show God as ultimately just, even though he allows injustice both positively and negatively in THIS age?

Job: The Cry of the Righteous Sufferer

How does the gospel require that the innocent may suffer unjustly?

A Possibility

As Job begins to probe the hypotheticals, a small hole in the fabric of Retribution Theology begins to emerge. Could it be possible for God to be perfectly just and still allow an innocent to suffer in this life?

> **14** How then can I answer him
> or choose my arguments against him?
> **15** Even if I were in the right, I could not answer.
> I could only beg my Judge for mercy.
> **16** If I summoned him and he answered me,
> I do not believe he would pay attention to what I said.
> **17** He batters me with a whirlwind
> and multiplies my wounds without cause.
> **18** He doesn't let me catch my breath
> but fills me with bitter experiences.
> **19** If it is a matter of strength, look, he is the powerful one!
> If it is a matter of justice, who can summon him?
> **20** Even if I were in the right, my own mouth would condemn me;
> if I were blameless, my mouth would declare me guilty.

What repeated phrase in vv.15 and 20 begins to reveal this possibility?

If Job is innocent, why do you think he says in v.20 that his mouth would still condemn him?

Even if innocent, what does he seem to conclude in v.15 is his only real option?

Round One: Bildad V. Job

The Hopeless Defense
Though Job hints that he is convinced of his own innocence, he still seems overwhelmed by the prospect of launching a real appeal to God. That still seems a hopeless impossibility:

> 21 Though I am blameless,
> I no longer care about myself;
> I renounce my life.
> 22 It is all the same. Therefore I say,
> "He destroys both the blameless and the wicked."
> 23 When catastrophe brings sudden death,
> he mocks the despair of the innocent.
> 24 The earth is handed over to the wicked;
> he blindfolds its judges.
> If it isn't he, then who is it?
> 25 My days fly by faster than a runner;
> they flee without seeing any good.
> 26 They sweep by like boats made of papyrus,
> like an eagle swooping down on its prey.
> 27 If I said, "I will forget my complaint,
> change my expression, and smile,"
> 28 I would still live in terror of all my pains.
> I know you will not acquit me.
> 29 Since I will be found guilty,
> why should I struggle in vain?
> 30 If I wash myself with snow,
> and cleanse my hands with lye,
> 31 then you dip me in a pit of mud,
> and my own clothes despise me!
> 32 For he is not a man like me, that I can answer him,
> that we can take each other to court.

What does Job give in v.32 as the problem that prevents his appeal?

Job: The Cry of the Righteous Sufferer

The Missing Mediator
As Job expounds briefly on this problem, he begins to set the stage for one of the great gospel truths we glean from his struggle. Man needs a mediator between him and God:

> **33** There is no mediator between us,
> to lay his hand on both of us.
> **34** Let him take his rod away from me
> so his terror will no longer frighten me.
> **35** Then I would speak and not fear him.
> But that is not the case; I am on my own.

Given his place on God's redemptive timeline, how is Job's assessment here correct?

To what (and whom) does this predicament look forward?

The Appeal (Anyway)
Despite his claims that it is hopeless, Job's frustration compels him to speak as though he will appeal to God anyway. Sometimes in question, sometimes in bold petition, Job once again turns from speaking to his friend to address the God that has remained silent:

> **Job 10:1-22**
> **1** I am disgusted with my life.
> I will give vent to my complaint
> and speak in the bitterness of my soul.
> **2** I will say to God,
> "Do not declare me guilty!
> Let me know why you prosecute me.
> **3** Is it good for you to oppress,
> to reject the work of your hands,
> and favor the plans of the wicked?
> **4** Do you have eyes of flesh,
> or do you see as a human sees?

Round One: Bildad V. Job

5 Are your days like those of a human,
or your years like those of a man,
6 that you look for my iniquity
and search for my sin,
7 even though you know that I am not wicked
and that there is no one who can rescue from your power?
8 "Your hands shaped me and formed me.
Will you now turn and destroy me?
9 Please remember that you formed me like clay.
Will you now return me to dust?
10 Did you not pour me out like milk
and curdle me like cheese?
11 You clothed me with skin and flesh,
and wove me together with bones and tendons.
12 You gave me life and faithful love,
and your care has guarded my life.
13 "Yet you concealed these thoughts in your heart;
I know that this was your hidden plan:
14 if I sin, you would notice,
and would not acquit me of my iniquity.
15 If I am wicked, woe to me!
And even if I am righteous, I cannot lift up my head.
I am filled with shame
and have drunk deeply of my affliction.
16 If I am proud, you hunt me like a lion
and again display your miraculous power against me.
17 You produce new witnesses against me
and multiply your anger toward me.
Hardships assault me, wave after wave.
18 "Why did you bring me out of the womb?
I should have died and never been seen.
19 I wish I had never existed
but had been carried from the womb to the grave.
20 Are my days not few? Stop it!
Leave me alone, so that I can smile a little
21 before I go to a land of darkness and gloom,
never to return.
22 It is a land of blackness like the deepest darkness,
gloomy and chaotic,
where even the light is like the darkness."

Job: The Cry of the Righteous Sufferer

How does Job still acknowledge not only God's power but his goodness?

What does Job seem to want from God?

Reflection on the Second Exchange
Twice now Job has been unjustly charged with guilt by the friends who speak to him face to face. He has responded to them in both cases and then addressed the God he cannot see. He meets with frustration in both exchanges, and we begin to notice a desire for a sympathetic audience and especially for a sympathetic mediator. If only there were some man who could both know Job's innocence and plead his case to God! But what man could mediate this way? As Job asked, "How can a man be justified before God?" Who could be sympathetic as man to man yet still be qualified to appeal directly as God to God?

How does Job's yearning for a mediator anticipate the gospel and the work of Christ?

Paul argues in Rm 3:25 that God "passed over the sins previously committed" and then argues that justification by faith was available even before the law was given (4:13) and long before Christ came to atone for those sins as our perfect mediator (1 Tm 2:5; Heb 8:6; 9:15).

What does this say about Job's ability to be justified even all these centuries before the Christ?

Lesson 7 Dialogue: Round One: Zophar V. Job (Chs.11 - 14)

Zophar's Assessment

Job's friends continue to pile on. Zophar now chimes in, and just as his friends did, he too follows his Retribution Theology to the logical conclusion that Job (and his children) must have sinned to cause this suffering. If only Job will repent, then God will surely peal back the clouds and bring the sunshine again.

Shock (Zophar's, and probably ours)

Job 11:1–12
1 Then Zophar the Naamathite replied:

> 2 Should this abundance of words go unanswered
> and such a talker be acquitted?
> 3 Should your babbling put others to silence,
> so that you can keep on ridiculing
> with no one to humiliate you?
> 4 You have said, "My teaching is sound,
> and I am pure in your sight."
> 5 But if only God would speak
> and open his lips against you!
> 6 He would show you the secrets of wisdom,
> for true wisdom has two sides.
> Know then that God has chosen to overlook some of your iniquity.
>
> 7 Can you fathom the depths of God
> or discover the limits of the Almighty?
> 8 They are higher than the heavens—what can you do?
> They are deeper than Sheol—what can you know?
> 9 Their measure is longer than the earth
> and wider than the sea.
>
> 10 If he passes by and throws someone in prison
> or convenes a court, who can stop him?
> 11 Surely he knows which people are worthless.
> If he sees iniquity, will he not take note of it?
> 12 But a stupid person will gain understanding
> as soon as a wild donkey is born a human!

Job: The Cry of the Righteous Sufferer

Zophar directly attacks Job's speech. The word "talker" in v.2 literally means "man of lips." Remember how the narrator told us in 2:10 that Job "did not sin in what he said." That literally translates as "with his lips," the same term. Zophar further calls Job's speech "babbling" and "ridiculing." We wonder whether Zophar sees Job as ridiculing his friends, or ridiculing God. In the latter case, especially given the strong legal language of "acquitted," Zophar's accusation seems to directly contradict the inspired narrator's assertion, or else there has been a change in Job's behavior since 2:10.

Have you seen evidence thus far that Job has sinned against God in his speech?

Zophar paints Job's defense as a caricature in v.4, for Job had not claimed to be pure but only innocent. The doubling of wisdom in v.6 – "two sides" – has been difficult to translate, but the idea seems to be that true wisdom is greater than man's understanding of it. That Zophar would accuse Job of asserting to have complete understanding about his situation is highly ironic, since Job is clearly struggling to make sense of this.

Christian finance guru, Dave Ramsey, is known for his typical response to polite greetings. When asked, "How are you?" he usually responds, "Better than I deserve." This appears to be Zophar's assessment of Job in v.6, that Job is getting better than he deserves. Bildad had concluded Job's children were dead because they deserved it (8:4), but apparently God has extended more mercy to Job.

In what sense is it true that Job has gotten better than he deserves? In what sense does Zophar have that totally wrong?

In vv.7-12 Zophar rehearses what Job has freely admitted, that God's wisdom and power are ultimate, far above any mere human. Then he excoriates Job with his implicit character assassination in vv.11-12 with his talk about "worthless" and "stupid" people whom he associates with a "wild donkey." Wow. No wonder Job is so desperate for a sympathetic mediator!

Advice
Apparently, Zophar's great "compassion" is coupled with great "wisdom," so he generously shares his "loving" advice for his friend Job:

Round One: Zophar V. Job

13 As for you, if you redirect your heart
and spread out your hands to him in prayer—
14 if there is iniquity in your hand, remove it,
and don't allow injustice to dwell in your tents—
15 then you will hold your head high, free from fault.
You will be firmly established and unafraid.
16 For you will forget your suffering,
recalling it only as water that has flowed by.
17 Your life will be brighter than noonday;
its darkness will be like the morning.
18 You will be confident, because there is hope.
You will look carefully about and lie down in safety.
19 You will lie down with no one to frighten you,
and many will seek your favor.
20 But the sight of the wicked will fail.
Their way of escape will be cut off,
and their only hope is their last breath.

Once again, there is a clear presumption of guilt on Job's part. He would have no need to "redirect" his heart unless it were amiss. The "if" in v.14 is surely intended as a "since." Notice that vv.13-14 accurately reflect the definition of "integrity" from the prologue, that it involves not only one's heart but also one's interpersonal actions. So, Zophar advises Job to get his heart right and to correct any injustices he has perpetrated on others. Then his future will be so bright that his "darkness will be like the morning"!

What do the terms "unafraid" (v.15), "frighten" (v.19) and "safety" (v.18) tell us about Zophar's definition of blessing?

What does the statement "many will seek your favor" tell us about Zophar's picture of Job's status if everything is back the way it should be?

Job: The Cry of the Righteous Sufferer

Job's Response
Sarcasm and His Own Shock

> **Job 12**
> **1** Then Job answered:
>
> **2** No doubt you are the people,
> and wisdom will die with you!
> **3** But I also have a mind like you;
> I am not inferior to you.
> Who doesn't know the things you are talking about?
>
> **4** I am a laughingstock to my friends,
> by calling on God, who answers me.
> The righteous and blameless man is a laughingstock.
> **5** The one who is at ease holds calamity in contempt
> and thinks it is prepared for those whose feet are slipping.
> **6** The tents of robbers are safe,
> and those who trouble God are secure;
> God holds them in his hands.

Job bites back with sarcasm. His friends are smug, like backup quarterbacks watching tape on Monday to criticize the starter who still sports his battle wounds from the 400-pound defensive linemen who repeatedly sacked him on Sunday. Notice the contrast between Job, the "righteous and blameless man," and his friends, first collectively, and then singularly, "the one who is at ease." His friends are ignorant that he is innocent, yet they talk down to him as though *he* is the ignorant one, as though he doesn't know that God is sovereign over his suffering.

It seems ridiculous that Job is a "laughingstock" (2x in v.4) for calling on God, when his friends have prescribed that he does exactly that. From their view, the problem is that he is calling out for answers (because he is innocent and confused) rather than for forgiveness. They think calamity is prepared only for those who do wrong, those "whose feet are slipping." Job declares that things are upside down. The wicked – the "robbers" and "those who trouble God" – are secure, while he suffers without cause.

Common Knowledge
His friends are not so smart. They cannot explain this reversal for Job. All they can do is come up with accusations against him. Everyone is in God's hands (v.6), and subject to his wisdom and strength (v.13 below). Job goes on to sass them for stating the obvious:

Round One: Zophar V. Job

7 But ask the animals, and they will instruct you;
ask the birds of the sky,
and they will tell you.
8 Or speak to the earth, and it will instruct you;
let the fish of the sea inform you.
9 Which of all these does not know
that the hand of the LORD has done this?
10 The life of every living thing is in his hand,
as well as the breath of all humanity.
11 Doesn't the ear test words
as the palate tastes food?
12 Wisdom is found with the elderly,
and understanding comes with long life.
13 Wisdom and strength belong to God;
counsel and understanding are his.
14 Whatever he tears down cannot be rebuilt;
whoever he imprisons cannot be released.
15 When he withholds water, everything dries up,
and when he releases it, it destroys the land.
16 True wisdom and power belong to him.
The deceived and the deceiver are his.
17 He leads counselors away barefoot
and makes judges go mad.
18 He releases the bonds put on by kings
and fastens a belt around their waists.
19 He leads priests away barefoot
and overthrows established leaders.
20 He deprives trusted advisers of speech
and takes away the elders' good judgment.
21 He pours out contempt on nobles
and disarms the strong.
22 He reveals mysteries from the darkness
and brings the deepest darkness into the light.
23 He makes nations great, then destroys them;
he enlarges nations, then leads them away.
24 He deprives the world's leaders of reason,
and makes them wander in a trackless wasteland.
25 They grope around in darkness without light;
he makes them stagger like a drunkard.

Job: The Cry of the Righteous Sufferer

This high view of God's sovereign power over his creatures is not unique to Job's three friends. It is common knowledge for everyone, great to small. Notice once again that from this view Job sees his trouble as coming from the "hand of the Lord" (v.9). His assertion is true only in the sense that God has sovereignly *allowed* it, but it is stated in ignorance of the satanic opponent directly responsible for *causing* it. Without that knowledge, Job's perspective is objectively equal to that of his friends:

Job 13

> **1** Look, my eyes have seen all this;
> my ears have heard and understood it.
> **2** Everything you know, I also know;
> I am not inferior to you.

The Preferred Appeal

Rather than being inferior, Job's knowledge is actually *better* informed than that of his friends. He knows internally what they cannot, that he has not caused this calamity by some moral lapse. Because of this gap between his perspective and theirs, there is no use in appealing to them, as they repeatedly prove. That pushes Job back to only one other option, as hopeless as it seems. He would prefer to speak to God, and he explains why:

> **3** Yet I prefer to speak to the Almighty
> and argue my case before God.
> **4** You use lies like plaster;
> you are all worthless healers.
> **5** If only you would shut up
> and let that be your wisdom!
> **6** Hear now my argument,
> and listen to my defense.
> **7** Would you testify unjustly on God's behalf
> or speak deceitfully for him?
> **8** Would you show partiality to him
> or argue the case in his defense?
> **9** Would it go well if he examined you?
> Could you deceive him as you would deceive a man?
> **10** Surely he would rebuke you
> if you secretly showed partiality.
> **11** Would God's majesty not terrify you?
> Would his dread not fall on you?
> **12** Your memorable sayings are proverbs of ash;
> your defenses are made of clay.

Round One: Zophar V. Job

Risk and Hope

We had already seen that Job yearned for a mediator. It is clear here that he will find none among his three friends, for they are not qualified to speak on God's behalf nor Job's. It would be better if they would just shut up (v.5). His desperation continues to push him to boldness. He WILL appeal to God and defend his innocence and let the chips fall where they may:

> **13** Be quiet, and I will speak.
> Let whatever comes happen to me.
> **14** I will put myself at risk
> and take my life in my own hands.
> **15** Even if he kills me, I will hope in him.
> I will still defend my ways before him.
> **16** Yes, this will result in my deliverance,
> for no godless person can appear before him.
> **17** Pay close attention to my words;
> let my declaration ring in your ears.
> **18** Now then, I have prepared my case;
> I know that I am right.
> **19** Can anyone indict me?
> If so, I will be silent and die.

How does Job's statement, "Even if he kills me, I will hope in him," reflect on Job's integrity? On his desperation?

How have you seen desperation draw you or someone else close to God?

How does Job's question, "Would it go well if he examined you?" (v.9) help us to remain humble when others are suffering?

Job's Prayer

Job makes his appeal. He prays for a time-out, so he and God can talk this out:

Job: The Cry of the Righteous Sufferer

> **20** Only grant these two things to me, God,
> so that I will not have to hide from your presence:
> **21** remove your hand from me,
> and do not let your terror frighten me.
> **22** Then call, and I will answer,
> or I will speak, and you can respond to me.
> **23** How many iniquities and sins have I committed?
> Reveal to me my transgression and sin.
> **24** Why do you hide your face
> and consider me your enemy?
> **25** Will you frighten a wind-driven leaf?
> Will you chase after dry straw?
> **26** For you record bitter accusations against me
> and make me inherit the iniquities of my youth.
> **27** You put my feet in the stocks
> and stand watch over all my paths,
> setting a limit for the soles of my feet.
> **28** A person wears out like something rotten,
> like a moth-eaten garment.

Job desperately wants God to make this stop ("remove your hand" in v.21). He wants to sense God's nearness, because right now Job feels like he must "hide" (v.20) and also feels like God is "hiding" his good pleasure from him (v.24).

Have you ever been in a situation when you'd rather "take your lumps" than endure the "silent treatment"? For what is Job asking in vv.22-23?

Job breaks out in lament again, but this time venting to God himself:

> **Job 14**
>
> **1** Anyone born of woman is short of days and full of trouble.
> **2** He blossoms like a flower, then withers;
> he flees like a shadow and does not last.
> **3** Do you really take notice of one like this?
> Will you bring me into judgment against you?
> **4** Who can produce something pure from what is impure?
> No one!

Round One: Zophar V. Job

5 Since a person's days are determined
and the number of his months depends on you,
and since you have set limits he cannot pass,
6 look away from him and let him rest
so that he can enjoy his day like a hired worker.

7 There is hope for a tree:
If it is cut down, it will sprout again,
and its shoots will not die.
8 If its roots grow old in the ground
and its stump starts to die in the soil,
9 the scent of water makes it thrive
and produce twigs like a sapling.
10 But a person dies and fades away;
he breathes his last—where is he?
11 As water disappears from a lake
and a river becomes parched and dry,
12 so people lie down never to rise again.
They will not wake up until the heavens are no more;
they will not stir from their sleep.

13 If only you would hide me in Sheol
and conceal me until your anger passes.
If only you would appoint a time for me
and then remember me.
14 When a person dies, will he come back to life?
If so, I would wait all the days of my struggle
until my relief comes.
15 You would call, and I would answer you.
You would long for the work of your hands.
16 For then you would count my steps
but would not take note of my sin.
17 My rebellion would be sealed up in a bag,
and you would cover over my iniquity.
18 But as a mountain collapses and crumbles
and a rock is dislodged from its place,
19 as water wears away stones
and torrents wash away the soil from the land,
so you destroy a man's hope.
20 You completely overpower him, and he passes on;
you change his appearance and send him away.

Job: The Cry of the Righteous Sufferer

> **21** If his sons receive honor, he does not know it;
> if they become insignificant, he is unaware of it.
> **22** He feels only the pain of his own body
> and mourns only for himself.

Gospel Cravings

Job's lament draws to a close on a real downer: "You destroy a man's hope" (v.19). Still, somehow God's power to save keeps drawing Job forward. How does the gospel answer these cravings expressed by Job in this last chapter?

"Who can produce something pure from something impure?" (v.4)

"Let him rest." (v.6)

"If only you would appoint a time for me and then remember me." (v.13)

"When a person dies, will he come back to life?" (v.14)

"You would call, and I would answer you." (v.15)

"You would...not take note of my sin...and you would cover my iniquity." (vv.16-17)

Lesson 8 Dialogue: Round Two: Eliphaz V. Job (Chs.15 - 17)

As worn out as we may feel from the debates so far, that was only the first round for Job and his friends. Imagine how exhausted Job feels! Up to this point, all four men have operated from the same understanding of how things are supposed to work: God blesses the righteous, but he destroys the wicked. Still, Job and his friends are reaching very different conclusions about his current predicament. The friends have pat answers, all figuring that Job must have sin he needs to confess, and then everything will be better again. Job insists he is innocent of wrongdoing, and so he has no answers, only questions and angst.

One commentator summarizes that in round one Eliphaz had emphasized "the moral perfection of God, Bildad his unwavering justice, and Zophar his omniscience. Job in reply had dwelt on his own unmerited sufferings and declared his willingness to meet God face to face to argue his case." Job's companions did not change their minds about why Job was suffering and the larger issue of the basis of the divine-human relationship. They continued to hold the dogma of retribution. Their spirit did change, however, to one of greater hostility. They seem to have abandoned hope that direct appeals to Job would move him to repent because they no longer called on him to repent. Instead, they stressed the fate of the wicked and indirectly urged him to repent. In their first speeches their approach was more intellectual; they challenged Job to think logically. In their second speeches their approach was more emotional; they sought to convict Job's conscience."[9]

Eliphaz Gets More Direct

As before (and probably because he is oldest), Eliphaz starts this round of speeches:

> **Job 15**
> **1** Then Eliphaz the Temanite replied:
>
> > **2** Does a wise man answer with empty counsel
> > or fill himself with the hot east wind?
> > **3** Should he argue with useless talk
> > or with words that serve no good purpose?

We don't have to understand ancient idioms to get the drift here. Job is full of hot air and "empty counsel." He is not talking like a wise man. Benefit of the doubt is out the window. We've come a long way from 2:11, where it is said Job's friends came to "sympathize with [Job] and comfort him."

Before we get too judgy on Eliphaz, we need to remember he is likely well-intended. He almost surely sees himself as defending his (rightly) high view of God's righteousness. God cannot be to

---

[9] Constable, T. (2003). *Tom Constable's Expository Notes on the Bible* (Job 14:1). Galaxie Software.

blame for Job's misfortune. Remember, his theology doesn't offer any other cause for his friend's suffering than some kind of sin on Job's part. He is not wrong to be driven by truth, but his perception of truth is inadequate and erroneous. Even if he were right that Job were at fault somehow, surely as a friend he should be more inclined to win Job over in love.

Questioning that Threatens

From a counseling standpoint (given his goal from ch.2 to "sympathize" and "comfort"), Eliphaz's practical error is to emphasize the propositional over the personal. He is defending God as a doctrinal system, and he is treating Job as a threat to that doctrinal system rather than as his personal friend. He sees Job's protests of innocence as an attack on what is in his view a sound theological belief system, that of Retribution Theology. This leaves no room for Job to question God (or his three fine representatives currently debating on his behalf against Job). On Eliphaz's view, to question is to threaten:

> **4** But you even undermine the fear of God
> and hinder meditation before him.
> **5** Your iniquity teaches you what to say,
> and you choose the language of the crafty.
> **6** Your own mouth condemns you, not I;
> your own lips testify against you.

See how the rigid nature of Retribution Theology forces a cold and condemning response! Eliphaz has come as a good friend to console and comfort. But because his understanding of God's righteous rule is so narrow, he overreacts when Job cries out with questions.

Job's life is like an automobile that was purring along smoothly, but now suddenly won't run at all. In fact, flames have erupted from under the hood! Eliphaz (with the other mechanics) came to help. He has plugged his computer into the diagnostic port, but it has short-circuited straight to a faulty reading: it indicates with flashing red lights that Job has an integrity malfunction. Eliphaz gets this misdiagnosis because his diagnostic machine is missing an important update. Without that update, it cannot account for the fact that the vehicle was sabotaged by a third party. Somebody threw a nasty wrench in there or stuck a banana in the tailpipe!

We saw the villain perform the sabotage (twice). We have the theological update. That's why Job's story is recorded for us. From Job's perspective, he really needs a Master Mechanic to fix this. It seems like this thing will never run again. Even when it does in the end, as far as we can tell, Job will still not know what caused the breakdown. He can only shrug his shoulders and keep trusting his Master Mechanic knows what's up.

For now, we're still at the side of the road with Job and his broken-down life and his would-be mechanic. This mechanic is not Master certified, and he does not like anyone to insinuate that his

Round Two: Eliphaz V. Job

gear (his Retribution Theology) or his diagnosis could be wrong. Just like an "expert" whose assessment has been challenged, Eliphaz is getting really testy.

Have you ever seen people (even church leaders!) get testy when others have questioned their beliefs? What did that look like and how did it feel?

What does it communicate to outsiders if the church sounds like a place where questions are unwelcome?

Does it bother you to think you don't have all the answers in your own understanding of God and his Word? How do you handle it when theological questions arise in your own mind?

Eliphaz doesn't take Job's questions lightly. He takes them as attacks on God, a failure to fear or properly revere him. In this, Eliphaz now seems to regard Job as not only *foolish* but *dangerous*. The kinds of things he has been saying are a threat to society, as they promote bad doctrine, he thinks.

How do people today characterize others as dangerous because of their religious speech?

How have non-Christians begun to characterize Christians as dangerous in this way?

Eliphaz's accusations of vv.4-6 seem to completely disregard his history with his friend, whom he earlier lauded as a spiritual leader and teacher (4:3-4). Before, he treated him as one who was overwhelmed and not acting like himself. Now he seems to accuse him of being a crafty fraud, as though his righteousness had been a show (15:5). So, Eliphaz responds with questions of his own, questions meant to intimidate and put Job back in his place:

Job: The Cry of the Righteous Sufferer

Threatening Questions

> **7** Were you the first human ever born,
> or were you brought forth before the hills?
> **8** Do you listen in on the council of God,
> or have a monopoly on wisdom?
> **9** What do you know that we don't?
> What do you understand that is not clear to us?
> **10** Both the gray-haired and the elderly are with us—
> older than your father.
> **11** Are God's consolations not enough for you,
> even the words that deal gently with you?
> **12** Why has your heart misled you,
> and why do your eyes flash
> **13** as you turn your anger against God
> and allow such words to leave your mouth?
> **14** What is a mere human, that he should be pure,
> or one born of a woman, that he should be righteous?
> **15** If God puts no trust in his holy ones
> and the heavens are not pure in his sight,
> **16** how much less one who is revolting and corrupt,
> who drinks injustice like water?

How does Eliphaz characterize Job in vv.12-16?

How do his remarks in vv.5-6 directly contradict 2:10 and 1:22 (that Job did not sin in his speech or by blaming God)?

The "mechanic," sure of his diagnosis, drones on with his expert opinion once again. This time, he doesn't even seem aimed at fixing the problem. He's more like the angry father preaching at the irresponsible son for ruining his car by neglect. Job has apparently done worse than miss oil changes and radiator flushes. The way Eliphaz talks, Job has been driving like a demon off-road and into brick walls, hell-bent on destroying this car and blaming it on the manufacturer.

Round Two: Eliphaz V. Job

Warnings About the Wicked (Read: Job)

17 Listen to me and I will inform you.
I will describe what I have seen,
18 what the wise have declared and not concealed,
that came from their ancestors,
19 to whom alone the land was given
when no foreigner passed among them.
20 A wicked person writhes in pain all his days,
throughout the number of years reserved for the ruthless.
21 Dreadful sounds fill his ears;
when he is at peace, a robber attacks him.
22 He doesn't believe he will return from darkness;
he is destined for the sword.
23 He wanders about for food, asking, "Where is it?"
He knows the day of darkness is at hand.
24 Trouble and distress terrify him,
overwhelming him like a king prepared for battle.
25 For he has stretched out his hand against God
and has arrogantly opposed the Almighty.
26 He rushes headlong at him
with his thick, studded shields.
27 Though his face is covered with fat
and his waistline bulges with it,
28 he will dwell in ruined cities,
in abandoned houses destined to become piles of rubble.
29 He will no longer be rich; his wealth will not endure.
His possessions will not increase in the land.
30 He will not escape from the darkness;
flames will wither his shoots,
and by the breath of God's mouth, he will depart.
31 Let him not put trust in worthless things, being led astray,
for what he gets in exchange will prove worthless.
32 It will be accomplished before his time,
and his branch will not flourish.
33 He will be like a vine that drops its unripe grapes
and like an olive tree that sheds its blossoms.
34 For the company of the godless will have no children,
and fire will consume the tents of those who offer bribes.
35 They conceive trouble and give birth to evil;
their womb prepares deception.

Job: The Cry of the Righteous Sufferer

What do you suppose Job is to conclude with all Eliphaz's remarks about the "wicked" and "godless"?

If Eliphaz gave Job any benefit of the doubt at first, how does he characterize him now in v.25?

Job Responds
Trading Places
If round two is characterized by emotional escalation, Job keeps pace as he responds. He makes a quick jab back at his friend, accusing him of his own vacuous speech. Further, he asserts that were the tables turned, he would be much more understanding and helpful than Eliphaz:

Job 16
1 Then Job answered:

> 2 I have heard many things like these.
> You are all miserable comforters.
> 3 Is there no end to your empty words?
> What provokes you that you continue testifying?
> 4 If you were in my place I could also talk like you.
> I could string words together against you
> and shake my head at you.
> 5 Instead, I would encourage you with my mouth,
> and the consolation from my lips would bring relief.

What do you suppose makes Job think he'd be more consoling and encouraging than his friend is? How much do you think that has to do with what he is going through?

How does Job here remind us that it is easier to judge and condemn than to listen and encourage?

Round Two: Eliphaz V. Job

How have your own struggles prepared you to be more understanding and sympathetic with others when they are having a hard time?

Targeted by God and the Wicked

Having fired a shot back at his friend, Job retreats again into expressing his agony. We can feel his confusion as he goes back and forth, speaking *about* God and then *to* God. It's as if he blindly cries out into the dark, not sure or caring to whom:

> **6** If I speak, my suffering is not relieved,
> and if I hold back, does any of it leave me?
> **7** Surely he has now exhausted me.
> You have devastated my entire family.
> **8** You have shriveled me up—it has become a witness;
> my frailty rises up against me and testifies to my face.
> **9** His anger tears at me, and he harasses me.
> He gnashes his teeth at me.
> My enemy pierces me with his eyes.
> **10** They open their mouths against me
> and strike my cheeks with contempt;
> they join themselves together against me.
> **11** God hands me over to the unjust;
> he throws me to the wicked.
> **12** I was at ease, but he shattered me;
> he seized me by the scruff of the neck
> and smashed me to pieces.
> He set me up as his target;
> **13** his archers surround me.
> He pierces my kidneys without mercy
> and pours my bile on the ground.
> **14** He breaks through my defenses again and again;
> he charges at me like a warrior.

Clearly, still unaware of the satanic sabotage, Job continues to see himself as God's target. Worse, he is a military target of a warrior and his sharpshooters. Job is keenly aware of his frailty (v.8), like a soldier out in the open with no cover. God is an angry enemy that "gnashes" at him and "pierces him" (v.9). His enemy also includes those who mock him (v.10). This crowd is made up of the "unjust" and the "wicked" (v.11). Job here is probably alluding to the reversal of the way

Job: The Cry of the Righteous Sufferer

things ought to be, that he who is righteous is being mocked by the wicked who are not suffering. This may well also be a jab at his friends who are treating him unjustly.

A Speck of Hope Wrapped in Despair

Job's reactions to this attack are complex. He initially seems resigned to his fate, but even then, is protesting his innocence. There is a faint speck of hope, too. Job appeals to the earth to leave his case exposed, demanding resolution just like the blood of Abel demanded justice (Gn 4:10). For his own justice, Job's appeal must lift to heaven:

> **15** I have sewn sackcloth over my skin;
> I have buried my strength in the dust.
> **16** My face has grown red with weeping,
> and darkness covers my eyes,
> **17** although my hands are free from violence
> and my prayer is pure.
> **18** Earth, do not cover my blood;
> may my cry for help find no resting place.
> **19** Even now my witness is in heaven,
> and my advocate is in the heights!
> **20** My friends scoff at me
> as I weep before God.
> **21** I wish that someone might argue for a man with God
> just as anyone would for a friend.
> **22** For only a few years will pass
> before I go the way of no return.

Job 17

> **1** My spirit is broken.
> My days are extinguished.
> A graveyard awaits me.

To whom do you think Job is referring as his "witness" and his "advocate" in v.19? How does this look forward to the ministry of Jesus Christ?

For what does Job wish in v.21? How does this anticipate the work of Christ?

Round Two: Eliphaz V. Job

Security, Scorn and Strength

Job's heart keeps crying out for what the gospel will one day answer. Since his friends only mock him, he needs someone who will represent him and ensure fair judgment:

> **2** Surely mockers surround me,
> and my eyes must gaze at their rebellion.
> **3** Accept my pledge! Put up security for me.
> Who else will be my sponsor?
> **4** You have closed their minds to understanding,
> therefore you will not honor them.
> **5** If a man denounces his friends for a price,
> the eyes of his children will fail.

Constable helps us understand the legal language of "security" here:

> "Evidently in legal cases of this sort each litigant would give the judge a bond (money or some personal possession) before the trial. This bond would guarantee that the litigant would be fair and honest during the trial. If one of the litigants was not, the judge would not return his bond to him at the trial's end. Job called on God to lay down His pledge (as the prosecutor) with Himself (the judge; 17:3a). The guarantor (17:3b) was one who provided the bond if the person on trial could not. Job's supportive friends would normally have provided his bond, but they had turned against him. Job lay the ultimate responsibility for his friends' blindness and rejection at God's feet because God had withheld understanding from them. Consequently, he believed God would not lift them up (17:4)."[10]

Job's friends weren't the only ones to scorn him by treating him unfairly:

> **6** He has made me an object of scorn to the people;
> I have become a man people spit at.
> **7** My eyes have grown dim from grief,
> and my whole body has become but a shadow.
> **8** The upright are appalled at this,
> and the innocent are roused against the godless.
> **9** Yet the righteous person will hold to his way,
> and the one whose hands are clean will grow stronger.
> **10** But come back and try again, all of you.
> I will not find a wise man among you.

---

[10] Constable, T. (2003). *Tom Constable's Expository Notes on the Bible* (Job 17:3). Galaxie Software.

Job: The Cry of the Righteous Sufferer

The way vv.8-10 fit into this speech is notoriously difficult. It may be helpful to understand Job as being sarcastic once again. His friends are taking the position of the "upright" by being appalled at Job's situation, but not the way they should. They see themselves as the "innocent" being "roused against the godless" (Job). Despite this, Job, who is actually "the righteous person" will "hold to his way" and in fact "will grow stronger."

Taken this way, Job is acting much like Rocky Balboa in the "Rocky" movies. More than once, when the prizefighter was nearly beaten to a pulp by his imposing opponents, he would somehow dig deep for a reserve of resolve and spring to life with a renewed energy. With his "eye of the tiger" he'd dare his nemesis, "Come on, hit me!" He'd drop his defenses and dare the opponent to give him his best shot, which they invariably did, and more than once. Then, Rocky would spring back with a retaliation they could not withstand.

Job seems to offer his own version: "Come back and try again, all of you." It seems he is again expressing his confidence that none of his detractors can draw from their "wisdom" any evidence that Job has given up his integrity.

Well, if there is a flash of determination in that outburst, it is quickly swallowed up again in the blood and sweat of the prizefighter hitting the floor in exhaustion. He anticipates the dimming view of his final knockout:

> **11** My days have slipped by;
> my plans have been ruined,
> even the things dear to my heart.
> **12** They turned night into day
> and made light seem near in the face of darkness.
> **13** If I await Sheol as my home,
> spread out my bed in darkness,
> **14** and say to corruption, "You are my father,"
> and to the maggot, "My mother" or "My sister,"
> **15** where then is my hope?
> Who can see any hope for me?
> **16** Will it go down to the gates of Sheol,
> or will we descend together to the dust?

Round Two: Eliphaz V. Job

Reflection

How does the gospel give us security, knowing our undeserved suffering will be noticed and vindicated by God?

How does our gospel living bring undeserved scorn from others?

How does the indwelling Spirit of Christ provide our reserve of strength in the knockout moments of our lives?

Lesson 9 Dialogue: Round Two: Bildad V. Job (Chs.18 - 19)

Bildad Gets Even More Indignant

Job, like a champion prizefighter, has been dealt blow after blow. It's bad enough to get repeatedly clocked by an opponent he can't even see. Job continues to talk like that invisible foe is God. We understand that the foe was Satan, not God. We realize that God is the ringmaster who has *allowed* these blows (though they strike us as being below the belt), but God is not Job's foe.

On top of the devastation from his unseen opponent, Job is taking blows from visible opponents too. His friends came to sympathize with him, but once the speeches started, their theology has diverted their energy to judgment and away from sympathy, like an irrigation valve sending water into a flood zone while parched soil blows away in the wind. These guys can't seem to help themselves. They don't really offer any new insights in round two, but they are escalating their responses.

Since Eliphaz seemed to nudge Job not one bit with his second speech, Bildad takes another crack at it. He just cannot believe Job's stubbornness, nor his defense of his position.

Who Do You Think You Are?

Job has wished he had someone qualified to mediate between him and God. Someone who could sympathize with him as a man but still somehow have the clout to approach God. Job's friends *could* sympathize with him as fellow men, but to Job's despair, they do not seem to do so. Bildad is more than perplexed by Job's protests and his cries for a sympathetic mediator. He is indignant (presumably on behalf of God and of righteousness). How could Job talk this way, when he clearly is in the wrong?

> **Job 18**
> **1** Then Bildad the Shuhite replied:
>
> **2** How long until you stop talking?
> Show some sense, and then we can talk.
> **3** Why are we regarded as cattle,
> as stupid in your sight?
> **4** You who tear yourself in anger—
> should the earth be abandoned on your account,
> or a rock be removed from its place?

What clues do we have here that Bildad's indignance is probably more in defense of his own position, wisdom, and reputation than on behalf of God or righteousness?

Job: The Cry of the Righteous Sufferer

Bildad is offended. He essentially voices mashups of two classics: "Who do you think you are?" and "What are we – chopped liver?" This debate now is much less about objective propositions and more about offended persons. Pride rears its ugly head. It may be worth noting that though Job alternates between speech directed at his friends and at God, his friends do not. They address only Job. Job's pride rises up when refuting his friends, but he seems to take a humbler tone with God. They speak at Job as though they faithfully represent God's position but give no evidence that they are appealing to God, whether about their assessments or in petition for their friend.

The Wicked and Unjust Man
Bildad launches yet another not-so-subtle tirade about the wicked man, with whom Job is surely supposed to identify himself:

> **5** Yes, the light of the wicked is extinguished;
> the flame of his fire does not glow.
> **6** The light in his tent grows dark,
> and the lamp beside him is put out.
> **7** His powerful stride is shortened,
> and his own schemes trip him up.
> **8** For his own feet lead him into a net,
> and he strays into its mesh.
> **9** A trap catches him by the heel;
> a noose seizes him.
> **10** A rope lies hidden for him on the ground,
> and a snare waits for him along the path.
> **11** Terrors frighten him on every side
> and harass him at every step.
> **12** His strength is depleted;
> disaster lies ready for him to stumble.
> **13** Parts of his skin are eaten away;
> death's firstborn consumes his limbs.
> **14** He is ripped from the security of his tent
> and marched away to the king of terrors.
> **15** Nothing he owned remains in his tent.
> Burning sulfur is scattered over his home.
> **16** His roots below dry up,
> and his branches above wither away.
> **17** All memory of him perishes from the earth;
> he has no name anywhere.
> **18** He is driven from light to darkness
> and chased from the inhabited world.

Round Two: Bildad V. Job

> **19** He has no children or descendants among his people,
> no survivor where he used to live.
> **20** Those in the west are appalled at his fate,
> while those in the east tremble in horror.
> **21** Indeed, such is the dwelling of the unjust man,
> and this is the place of the one who does not know God.

Bildad references "light" several times here (vv.5,6,18). This term can be used as a metaphor for life or vitality but can also carry the sense of wisdom, enlightenment, or vision. These amount to a package of blessing which seems to have escaped Job's grasp. Bildad implies that Job has turned from his previous enlightenment and wisdom and so has lost his vitality. He has stumbled in his darkness and gotten tripped up (vv.6-7).

Bildad uses another metaphor that is common in biblical wisdom literature, and this is a stronger accusation. He implies that Job is more than tripped up in the dark. He is caught in his own traps (vv.8-10). This is more than stumbling stupidity. This is getting what you have coming because you have schemed against others. Bildad paints Job as one who has plotted to take advantage of others for his own gain. For this reason, as surely as God is just, then Job was certain to find "terror...on every side" (v.11), weakness and disaster (v.12), disease and danger (vv.13-14), and total loss (vv.15-19). The devastation of this proverbial wicked man is shocking to people everywhere (v.20).

The accusations pile up into a peak with the final implication. At best, Bildad uses hyperbole to accuse Job of behaving *as though* he were such a wicked man. At worst, he speaks literally of Job as "one who does not know God."

What differences have you observed between people simply "stumbling in the dark" and those "scheming against others"?

Have you ever seen someone's wicked schemes blow back onto themselves? If so, what happened, and how did others see it?

Have you ever seen someone get blamed for a situation that was beyond their control or was due to the bad acting of others? How did that affect the innocent party or parties? How did others respond?

Job: The Cry of the Righteous Sufferer

Job Fires Back

It's Not About You
The more personal nature of this debate continues to be clear as Job responds:

> **Job 19**
> **1** Then Job answered:
> **2** How long will you torment me and crush me with words?
> **3** You have humiliated me ten times now,
> and you mistreat me without shame.
> **4** Even if it is true that I have sinned,
> my mistake concerns only me.

Job lets his friend know he has tormented, crushed, and humiliated him. In sum, he has shamelessly mistreated him. "Ten times now" is not a literal accounting but is a way of saying something is complete: "You have totally humiliated me."

Job uses the rhetorical technique of a hypothetical again: *Even if I am in the wrong, why is this such a big deal to YOU?* In v.4, Job is drawing out the fact we mentioned above, that Bildad acts as though he's offended on God's behalf. Job's point seems to be that God is capable of defending his own righteousness. Bildad's verdicts have no bearing. He can keep them to himself.

It is worth drawing out that the phrase "I have sinned" in v.4 is one word in the Hebrew (*sagiti*). This word often carries the nuance of *unconscious or unintentional error*. When God gave Moses the ceremonial law, this was the underlying idea of all the rituals for atonement. They presumed the general disposition of God's people was to intentionally follow God but that from time to time they would unwittingly or ignorantly sin. Once they became aware of their sin, they had to make atonement.

This same disposition was expressed about Job in chs.1-2, that he was wholehearted – expressing "complete integrity" and "turning away from evil" – in his desire to please God. Remember, it did not mean he was perfect, but that godliness was the consistent pattern of his intentions and actions. So, here in 19:4, he is not admitting to a willful turning away from God. At worst, he is only acknowledging, "Well, I'm not perfect, so it may be that I have offended God in some way I do not realize or intend. But even if that is so, that's not *your* problem, Bildad. I didn't do anything to *you*."

God Has Wronged Me
Job indicates that Bildad merely wants to appear superior to Job. He wants to exploit the luxury of his comfy Monday-morning-quarterback chair to sit and point and accuse, but he doesn't know what he's seeing on this game film. Job hasn't done this. God has:

Round Two: Bildad V. Job

5 If you really want to appear superior to me
and would use my disgrace as evidence against me,
6 then understand that it is God who has wronged me
and caught me in his net.

7 I cry out, "Violence!" but get no response;
I call for help, but there is no justice.
8 He has blocked my way so that I cannot pass through;
he has veiled my paths with darkness.
9 He has stripped me of my honor
and removed the crown from my head.
10 He tears me down on every side so that I am ruined.
He uproots my hope like a tree.
11 His anger burns against me,
and he regards me as one of his enemies.
12 His troops advance together;
they construct a ramp against me
and camp around my tent.
13 He has removed my brothers from me;
my acquaintances have abandoned me.
14 My relatives stop coming by,
and my close friends have forgotten me.
15 My house guests and female servants regard me as a stranger;
I am a foreigner in their sight.
16 I call for my servant, but he does not answer,
even if I beg him with my own mouth.
17 My breath is offensive to my wife,
and my own family finds me repulsive.
18 Even young boys scorn me.
When I stand up, they mock me.
19 All of my best friends despise me,
and those I love have turned against me.
20 My skin and my flesh cling to my bones;
I have escaped with only the skin of my teeth.

In Job's game of life, everything was going great. Winning record, blowout scores. Job was working hard as a disciplined player, heeding his Coach and sticking to the playbook. He even worked hard to keep the younger players in line. For his efforts, Job was piling up great stats and trophies ("honor" and "crown" in v.9), and he was a crowd favorite too ("brothers," "friends" and "guests" in vv.13-14).

Job: The Cry of the Righteous Sufferer

Then everything turned on a dime. Somehow the Coach's play calling left Job completely vulnerable. As he carried the ball, he hit a wall and couldn't find the gap (v.8). The opponents seemed to have a bullseye on him and came from all directions (v.12). Complete reversal. Suddenly, the violence of the game has overtaken him, and it seemed like even the Coach was against him (v.7)! He's lost his game face (v.10), his teammates and his fans. Now, Coach has sidelined him on the injured list (v.20).

Some understand Job in v.7 to be accusing God (the Coach) of being unjust in his treatment of him. This is probably taking the statement too strongly. There is presently a lack of vindication, but that does not mean God has wrongly judged Job. He has not judged him at all, for he has not spoken. Everything leaning that way has only been the verbalized conclusions of the friends, who presume to represent God. Officially, the verdict is still out until God speaks for himself (and he will). This explains why Job repeatedly appeals for that very event.

Have Mercy
How did this suddenly go so wrong? Job is understandably despondent. He appeals first to his teammates, his friends: *Come on, guys! Give me a break!*

> 21 Have mercy on me, my friends, have mercy,
> for God's hand has struck me.
> 22 Why do you persecute me as God does?
> Will you never get enough of my flesh?

Have you ever felt sidelined by God? Abandoned by friends? What was that like?

How does the cliché "When it rains, it pours" seem to ring true in these times?

Job's Great and Only Hope (and Ours)
In these next few verses Job expresses the heart of this dialogue and the core of his feeble but ferocious hope. It is a gospel conviction that is holy steam in the soul, fueling the unstoppable engine of life that carries a person along the tracks into the eternal future. Job's undying hope is to know his Redeemer face to face:

Round Two: Bildad V. Job

> **23** I wish that my words were written down,
> that they were recorded on a scroll
> **24** or were inscribed in stone forever
> by an iron stylus and lead!
> **25** But I know that my Redeemer lives,
> and at the end he will stand on the dust.
> **26** Even after my skin has been destroyed,
> yet I will see God in my flesh.
> **27** I will see him myself;
> my eyes will look at him, and not as a stranger.
> My heart longs within me.

The irony continues, for Job's words were indeed "written down" and were "recorded on a scroll" (possibly by himself). What's more, because they express the iron-clad truth of the gospel we now know to be realized in Jesus Christ, they are truly written "in stone." God has codified the truth spoken by Job, preserved it for generations of readers, including those like us who look back at the cross and resurrection and say, "Job, you were right! Your Redeemer DOES live, and his name is Jesus!"

Job seems to glimpse the end of this age, and God's coming in judgment, when he says, "at the end he will stand on the dust." This last term reminds mankind of what he is made. That God stands on the dust (or "earth") is a reminder that he is supreme over the earth and all its creatures, particularly man whom he made in his image. Job isn't explicit, but he may be developing a sense that God's justice may be found later, in this final judgment, rather than always coming to realization in one's earthly lifetime. This would blow the lid off the strict Retribution Theology of Job's friends (which he seems to have held as well).

Notice the apparent reference to bodily resurrection, though Job's understanding of that doctrine is surely not nearly as developed as that of the NT. While the core meaning of these verses is clear, there are notorious divisions about what Job is expressing regarding this resurrection hope. The point of disagreement is *when* Job thinks this event will transpire. Some maintain that Job still expects vindication in *this* life. This position is largely based on appeal to the end of the story, especially 42:5, and relies also on a general belief that the hope of personal (individual) resurrection is not present in the book, despite all that Job has said about the imminence of his death. Others, while admitting that the passage doesn't provide a full statement of faith in personal bodily resurrection, do find in it the hope of a favorable meeting with God *after death* as a genuine human being.

There are several good reasons for accepting the second position. First, there would be no need for Job to leave behind a written testimony (vv.23-24) if he expects to be vindicated before he dies. Second, the word translated *earth*, as used in Job, is constantly connected with Sheol, and the statement that the Redeemer *lives* is a direct answer to the fact that a man *dies* (14:10). The repetition of the word *after* (Heb. *ahar*) in the prominent position at the beginning of verses 25b ("at the end" is *aharon*) and 26a suggests an interval between Job's present moment and this event, an interval likely even spanning between Job's death and the end of this age. Finally, the argument that Job does not expect personal reconstitution as a man due to an undeveloped ancient perspective can be dismissed in the light of much recent research that shows interest in the afterlife as an ancient concern for Israelite faith. In particular, what we observed in such passages as Job 14:13ff., seem to show that the hope of resurrection lies at the very heart of Job's faith."[11] So, it seems very likely that Job is expressing an early and as yet undeveloped view of bodily resurrection. Job is certainly expressing personal sight of God, and it seems most likely he is also expressing bodily sight, and that it is experienced after Job's death.

The Sadducees, the religious leaders who were largely in power during Jesus' time (under Rome's authority), did *not* believe in the resurrection. It is no wonder they only accepted the first five books of the OT – the Torah – as authoritative. They would have had trouble dealing with Job regarding this point, let alone the Prophets. The Pharisees (which included Nicodemus and Paul) *did* believe in bodily resurrection, accepting the full OT witness and expressing this interest as Anderson says above. For Christians, the doctrine of resurrection was clearly expressed and fully developed in the NT, especially by Paul:

> **1 Corinthians 15:12–28**
> **12** Now if Christ is proclaimed as raised from the dead, how can some of you say, "There is no resurrection of the dead"? **13** If there is no resurrection of the dead, then not even Christ has been raised; **14** and if Christ has not been raised, then our proclamation is in vain, and so is your faith. **15** Moreover, we are found to be false witnesses about God, because we have testified wrongly about God that he raised up Christ—whom he did not raise up, if in fact the dead are not raised. **16** For if the dead are not raised, not even Christ has been raised. **17** And if Christ has not been raised, your faith is worthless; you are still in your sins. **18** Those, then, who have fallen asleep in Christ have also perished. **19** If we have put our hope in Christ for this life only, we should be pitied more than anyone.
>
> **20** But as it is, Christ has been raised from the dead, the firstfruits of those who have fallen asleep. **21** For since death came through a man, the resurrection of the dead also comes through a man. **22** For just as in Adam all die, so also in Christ all will be made alive.
>
> **23** But each in his own order: Christ, the firstfruits; afterward, at his coming, those who belong to Christ. **24** Then comes the end, when he hands over the kingdom to God the Father, when he abolishes all rule and all authority and power. **25** For he must reign until he puts all his enemies under his feet. **26** The last enemy to be abolished is death.

---

[11] Andersen, F. I. (1976). *Job: An Introduction and Commentary* (Vol. 14, pp. 209–210). Downers Grove, IL: InterVarsity Press.

Round Two: Bildad V. Job

> **27** For **God has put everything under his feet.** Now when it says "everything" is put under him, it is obvious that he who puts everything under him is the exception. **28** When everything is subject to Christ, then the Son himself will also be subject to the one who subjected everything to him, so that God may be all in all.

Job doesn't only look forward to seeing God. He anticipates this as a welcome and personal event. The phrase "and not as a stranger" (v.27) may mean that it is God that Job will see rather than someone else. Or it may refer to Job's reception then, that it will not be as a stranger, since it seems like God has been treating him as such of late. Both possibilities would fit the context, but Job's following statement of longing may favor the latter. Job places much confidence in the loving character of God, and he wants to experience it again.

Job seems to be looking beyond his mortal life for his vindication by a direct and personal encounter with God. In light of that powerful moment, he warns his friends (the "you" is plural) to be cautious about judging him harshly as they are doing:

> **Job 19:28-29**
> **28** If you say, "How will we pursue him,
> since the root of the problem lies with him?"
> **29** then be afraid of the sword,
> because wrath brings punishment by the sword,
> so that you may know there is a judgment.

Job's friends may be setting themselves up for God's judgment against *them*. This will actually turn out to the be the case in 42:7, though God only voices his anger but does not bring "the sword" upon them, choosing rather to allow Job to intercede on their behalf.

Job: The Cry of the Righteous Sufferer

Reflection on Seeing the Redeemer
How does the NT (e.g., 1 Cor 15 above) give us the clearer picture of Job's hope and ours?

Of the Redeemer?

Of God's judgment and vindication?

Of bodily resurrection?

How does Job in this chapter (19) point to the personal nature of Judgment Day, especially in vv.4, 27 and 29?

How is Job voicing the longing of every Christian? Of your personal longing?

Lesson 10 Dialogue: Round Two: Zophar V. Job (Chs.20 - 21)

Zophar Tries Again

Unsettling Thoughts and Insults

The debate has become more personal in Round Two. Zophar makes it clear when he speaks up again that he too is now more concerned with his own personal offense than with discussing the particular points of Job's defense.

> **Job 20**
> 1 Then Zophar the Naamathite replied:
>
> 2 This is why my unsettling thoughts compel me to answer,
> because I am upset!
> 3 I have heard a rebuke that insults me,
> and my understanding makes me reply.

Notice the clear connection. Why is Zophar upset? Because Job's rebuke insults him. The insult especially seems related to Zophar's understanding. He is apparently regarding Job as a smart aleck. Funny how perspectives turn around like that, isn't it? Irony abounds. Zophar is upset because he is personally offended, but that won't keep him from launching another tirade as though he is a disinterested party defending God's position rather than his own honor.

The Wicked Person's Lot from God

Quite predictably, this tirade offers Job yet another description of the wicked. Speech after speech, Job's friends rehearse their wisdom about God's antagonism toward the wicked, as though Job is not hearing them (or didn't already know such truths). Remember that old definition of insanity: *doing the same thing over and over and expecting different results.* To be fair, the other oldie-but-goodie has not yet been recorded: *Don't cast your pearls before swine.* They would surely see Job as the swine ignoring their pearls of wisdom, but Zophar keeps on casting all the same:

> 4 Don't you know that ever since antiquity,
> from the time a human was placed on earth,
> 5 the joy of the wicked has been brief
> and the happiness of the godless has lasted only a moment?
> 6 Though his arrogance reaches heaven,
> and his head touches the clouds,
> 7 he will vanish forever like his own dung.
> Those who know him will ask, "Where is he?"
> 8 He will fly away like a dream and never be found;
> he will be chased away like a vision in the night.

> **9** The eye that saw him will see him no more,
> and his household will no longer see him.
> **10** His children will beg from the poor,
> for his own hands must give back his wealth.
> **11** His frame may be full of youthful vigor,
> but it will lie down with him in dust.

What does Zophar imply about Job's situation in v.5? About his attitude in v.6?

About his future in vv.7-11?

In Round One (ch.11), Zophar told Job that if he would repent of his sin, his prospects were bright as the noonday! This time, he doesn't even bother with cheery possibilities, but only points to bleak certainties in colorful metaphors:

> **12** Though evil tastes sweet in his mouth
> and he conceals it under his tongue,
> **13** though he cherishes it and will not let it go
> but keeps it in his mouth,
> **14** yet the food in his stomach turns
> into cobras' venom inside him.
> **15** He swallows wealth but must vomit it up;
> God will force it from his stomach.
> **16** He will suck the poison of cobras;
> a viper's fangs will kill him.
> **17** He will not enjoy the streams,
> the rivers flowing with honey and curds.
> **18** He must return the fruit of his labor without consuming it;
> he doesn't enjoy the profits from his trading.
> **19** For he oppressed and abandoned the poor;
> he seized a house he did not build.

What does Zophar imply about Job's previous blessings in vv.18-19?

Round Two: Zophar V. Job

Zophar says the hard work of the wicked won't pay off, cursed much like Adam's work was after the rebellion in the Garden (Gn 3). The unjust oppressor will not be allowed to enjoy the would-be pleasures accumulated at the expense of the oppressed. A similar idea – that rebellion would cause the blessings of hard work to pass on to others who did not work for them – was bound up in God's decree of blessing and cursing with Israel as they prepared to enter the Promised Land (Dt 28).

Zophar implies that Job has found evil to be sweet to the taste, but that now it is turning his stomach like snake venom. He characterizes Job's current state, then, as a direct judgment of God (v.15). God's judgments were presented as sweet to the taste but bitter in the stomach to prophets Ezekiel (3:3) and John (Rv 10:9-10). Once again, Zophar expresses true and biblical ideas, but misapplies them in Job's case. This bitter season for Job is not God's judgment upon him. In ignorance of that fact, Zophar continues:

> **20** Because his appetite is never satisfied,
> he does not let anything he desires escape.
> **21** Nothing is left for him to consume;
> therefore, his prosperity will not last.
> **22** At the height of his success distress will come to him;
> the full weight of misery will crush him.
> **23** When he fills his stomach,
> God will send his burning anger against him,
> raining it down on him while he is eating.
> **24** If he flees from an iron weapon,
> an arrow from a bronze bow will pierce him.
> **25** He pulls it out of his back,
> the flashing tip out of his liver.
> Terrors come over him.
> **26** Total darkness is reserved for his treasures.
> A fire unfanned by human hands will consume him;
> it will feed on what is left in his tent.
> **27** The heavens will expose his iniquity,
> and the earth will rise up against him.
> **28** The possessions in his house will be removed,
> flowing away on the day of God's anger.
> **29** This is the wicked person's lot from God,
> the inheritance God ordained for him.

What does Zophar imply about Job's "appetite" and "desires"?

Job: The Cry of the Righteous Sufferer

What term does Zophar use (2x) to describe God's attitude toward the wicked, and what does that imply?

Job Responds
Bearing and Mocking
Job's responses continue to be more personal as well. But at least he is still offering objective propositional defense of his position. Still, his first reaction is emotional before it is rational. Once again, there is a sharp edge to his retort:

> **Job 21**
> 1 Then Job answered:
>
> 2 Pay close attention to my words;
> let this be the consolation you offer.
> 3 Bear with me while I speak;
> then after I have spoken, you may continue mocking.

Job seems to have abandoned the hope of sympathy. His only request now is that he gets a hearing from his friends (the "you" of v.2 is again plural). Since he can't get sympathy, this hearing will be his "consolation prize."

Why Shouldn't I Be Impatient?
If Zophar and the others will put a pin in the string of lofty speeches about the wicked, Job will offer evidence that things are not as simple as they would make it. He will present that case, and at the same time he will argue it is reasonable for him to be impatient with his situation:

> 4 As for me, is my complaint against a human being?
> Then why shouldn't I be impatient?
> 5 Look at me and shudder;
> put your hand over your mouth.
> 6 When I think about it, I am terrified
> and my body trembles in horror.
> 7 Why do the wicked continue to live,
> growing old and becoming powerful?
> 8 Their children are established while they are still alive,
> and their descendants, before their eyes.
> 9 Their homes are secure and free of fear;
> no rod from God strikes them.

Round Two: Zophar V. Job

> **10** Their bulls breed without fail;
> their cows calve and do not miscarry.
> **11** They let their little ones run around like lambs;
> their children skip about,
> **12** singing to the tambourine and lyre
> and rejoicing at the sound of the flute.
> **13** They spend their days in prosperity
> and go down to Sheol in peace.
> **14** Yet they say to God, "Leave us alone!
> We don't want to know your ways.
> **15** Who is the Almighty, that we should serve him,
> and what will we gain by pleading with him?"
> **16** But their prosperity is not of their own doing.
> The counsel of the wicked is far from me!

Job's friends keep insisting that God always makes sure the wicked are frustrated and cursed, while the godly cruise through life with no problems. He says: *Are you kidding me? Look around! There are lots of cases where the ungodly seem to have things going great!* One commentator points out that Job gives a description of the *wicked* in vv.7-13 that sounds more like the way Eliphaz described the life of the *righteous* man in 5:17-27! Zophar had just claimed the wicked die young (20:11), but Job contradicts him with the opposite assertion (v.13 above).

Job's observations here are much like those of the psalmist Asaph who was perplexed by this same phenomenon of the wicked getting undeserved blessing:

> **Psalm 73:1–14**
> **1** God is indeed good to Israel,
> to the pure in heart.
> **2** But as for me, my feet almost slipped;
> my steps nearly went astray.
> **3** For I envied the arrogant;
> I saw the prosperity of the wicked.
> **4** They have an easy time until they die,
> and their bodies are well fed.
> **5** They are not in trouble like others;
> they are not afflicted like most people.
> **6** Therefore, pride is their necklace,
> and violence covers them like a garment.
> **7** Their eyes bulge out from fatness;
> the imaginations of their hearts run wild.

Job: The Cry of the Righteous Sufferer

> **8** They mock, and they speak maliciously;
> they arrogantly threaten oppression.
> **9** They set their mouths against heaven,
> and their tongues strut across the earth.
> **10** Therefore his people turn to them
> and drink in their overflowing words.
> **11** The wicked say, "How can God know?
> Does the Most High know everything?"
> **12** Look at them—the wicked!
> They are always at ease,
> and they increase their wealth.
> **13** Did I purify my heart
> and wash my hands in innocence for nothing?
> **14** For I am afflicted all day long
> and punished every morning.

Asaph couldn't make sense of how good the wicked seem to have it. He wondered if he was a fool for remaining true to God. Then this psalm took a hard turn when his perspective was completely retuned. What made the change?

> **16** When I tried to understand all this,
> it seemed hopeless
> **17** until I entered God's sanctuary.
> Then I understood their destiny.

What gave Asaph perspective was God's presence. When Asaph came into God's sanctuary, he realized that the injustice he was noticing all around him was only temporary. Standing before the eternal God will give perspective. It did for Asaph, and it will for Job before his story is done.

How does injustice frustrate you when things don't seem to work out as they should?

How do times of privately and collectively coming into God's presence in worship help offset those times of frustration and disillusionment?

Round Two: Zophar V. Job

For now, Job is still looking around himself and wondering what gives. In fact, the explanation for how things can go so well for the wicked – even temporarily – is exactly *about* "what gives," or, more precisely, "Who gives." Job realizes in v.16 above, "their prosperity is not of their own doing."

This assessment hints at the truth we mentioned in an earlier lesson, a truth not accounted for in a strict Retribution Theology. God is so generous he gives grace even to the wicked. In theology, this is called *common grace*. This truth is expressed in the well-known saying of Jesus, "... he sends rain on the righteous and the unrighteous." Jesus is talking in an agrarian context about the blessing of rain that comes upon both types of people to cause growth and prosperity.

Job's point is that the wicked are not doing so well because they are earning blessing from God as a reward. They are merely enjoying God's generosity for a time. As Asaph noted back in Ps 73, this generosity will not last:

> **18** Indeed, you put them in slippery places;
> you make them fall into ruin.
> **19** How suddenly they become a desolation!
> They come to an end, swept away by terrors.
> **20** Like one waking from a dream,
> Lord, when arising, you will despise their image.

Job has not yet quite understood the bigger picture that Asaph did, but the sense of God's ultimate goodness and justice holds him. Job sticks with wisdom and keeps the counsel of the wicked far from himself (v.16). What he does not understand does not sway him from the God whose character he knows and trusts. Still, Job is frustrated by the injustice he sees, for it often goes well for the wicked:

This Life Does Not Reveal God's Justice (Always or Fully)

> **Job 21:17-22**
> **17** How often is the lamp of the wicked put out?
> Does disaster come on them?
> Does he apportion destruction in his anger?
> **18** Are they like straw before the wind,
> like chaff a storm sweeps away?
> **19** God reserves a person's punishment for his children.
> Let God repay the person himself, so that he may know it.
> **20** Let his own eyes see his demise;
> let him drink from the Almighty's wrath!
> **21** For what does he care about his family once he is dead,
> when the number of his months has run out?

Job: The Cry of the Righteous Sufferer

> **22** Can anyone teach God knowledge,
> since he judges the exalted ones?

Job's friends contend that even if the wicked seem to escape justice it is only briefly. Job's response amounts to this: *How many times have you seen it work out that way?* When the evidence of justice withheld is hard to dispute, perhaps the friends can punt: *If God doesn't bring retribution on so-and-so before he dies, then he can apply the punishment to so-and-so's children* (v.19a with 18:19 and 20:10). Job finds this appalling (19b-21), as did Jeremiah (31:29) and Ezekiel (18:2-3). As we mentioned in an earlier lesson, Jesus clearly debunked the idea that someone's suffering might be punishment for another's sins (Jn 9:1-3). So, that can't be the explanation of God's ultimate justice, that he shifts it to the wicked person's descendants.

Have you ever seen a child suffer because of a parent's actions? What were the consequences of that injustice?

Can you think of other examples of how we sometimes wrongly apply "guilt by association"?

What is the only biblical example of God's allowing a substitution, where his judgment and wrath are poured out on the innocent rather than the guilty? Why is this case so unique?

Once again, Job's friends miss the possibility that retribution may come after this life. Punishment must come to those deserving of it (apart from the substitutionary atonement of Jesus), and no one is accountable for the offenses of another. Job argues that God's judgment is beyond our simple formulations, for he even judges "the exalted ones" (v.22, probably a reference to angels). If God's judgment extends beyond this earth, it follows that it also extends beyond this mortal life.

Job goes on to speak of the great equalizer of death again:

> **23** One person dies in excellent health,
> completely secure and at ease.
> **24** His body is well fed,
> and his bones are full of marrow.

Round Two: Zophar V. Job

> **25** Yet another person dies with a bitter soul,
> having never tasted prosperity.
> **26** But they both lie in the dust,
> and worms cover them.
> **27** I know your thoughts very well,
> the schemes by which you would wrong me.
> **28** For you say, "Where now is the nobleman's house?"
> and "Where are the tents the wicked lived in?"
> **29** Have you never consulted those who travel the roads?
> Don't you accept their reports?
> **30** Indeed, the evil person is spared from the day of disaster,
> rescued from the day of wrath.
> **31** Who would denounce his behavior to his face?
> Who would repay him for what he has done?
> **32** He is carried to the grave,
> and someone keeps watch over his tomb.
> **33** The dirt on his grave is sweet to him.
> Everyone follows behind him,
> and those who go before him are without number.

Death comes to all, and injustice may extend even to the end of one's mortal life. It may be observed in this life in both positive and negative regards. Job sits in dust and ashes being accused by his friends and feeling abandoned by the God he serves wholeheartedly. At the same time, he sees the wicked doing just fine, some even all the way to the point of a seemingly sweet death (v.33). The simple formula of Retribution Theology applied to the limited scope of mortal life in this world surely cannot give a full account for the balance sheet of God's perfect justice...

> **34** So how can you offer me such futile comfort?
> Your answers are deceptive.

The view of Job's friends (Retribution Theology) is not nearly nuanced enough to account for these injustices in life. They tell Job to be pious in his heart and express justice in his dealings and everything will be great. They go on and on about how everything will be terrible for the wicked. They do not offer any explanation for why things are upside down in so many cases, nor why there is such a reversal now in Job's case. It is easier to point the finger at Job and ignore all the other anomalies. Job considers this approach of theirs worse than insensitive. It is deceptive.

What are some of the ways that people try to correct the injustices of this life?

Job: The Cry of the Righteous Sufferer

Does it seem like those human efforts will eventually prevail to bring justice to this world?

What does the Christian understand biblically as the only hope for living in a truly just world?

When and how does that perfect world come?

Lesson 11 Dialogue: Round Three: Eliphaz V. Job (Chs.22 - 24)

Job and his friends have exchanged blows for two rounds now, and no one has budged. What started with the best of intentions – three friends coming to commiserate with and console their friend – has dramatically shifted. Once the silence was broken by Job's initial lament, the three friends have maintained their position that Job (and all his children) must have sinned against God for all this to befall him. Job has argued that while he can't make sense of this either, he has not brought this on himself, and he is suffering unjustly.

All see this calamity as coming from God's hand, and all agree God cannot be charged with wrongdoing. The friends conclude the only other option to explain this misfortune is Job's wrongdoing, but Job scrambles for a third option, as yet unknown to any of them. (We readers know that third option to be multiple satanic attacks allowed by God for his purposes.) The friends were at first perplexed by Job's protests of innocence, but now that he has been unswayed by their persistent calls to repent, they are personally offended. The debate has really heated up!

Thus far Job has expressed some very powerful gospel cravings that are remarkable given his ancient, non-Israelite context. He has cried out for a mediator, one qualified to identify with him as man to man but also as God to God. This desire is for more than a mere hearing but also for redemption, for peace, and rest. Job fends off the blows of his friends and repeatedly turns to God asking for a chance to get some answers. He vacillates between despair and stubborn hopefulness. Surely, he cannot go on this way for long.

Eliphaz's Last Rebuke

So begins Round Three. Eliphaz starts in again. While he has been largely the most amenable and understanding of the three, it is now apparent that Job has exasperated even him. He seems to take Job's repeated deflections as sure evidence that Job has indeed been deeply guilty of sin:

No Difference to God

> **Job 22**
> **1** Then Eliphaz the Temanite replied:
>
> > **2** Can a man be of any use to God?
> > Can even a wise man be of use to him?
> > **3** Does it delight the Almighty if you are righteous?
> > Does he profit if you perfect your behavior?
> > **4** Does he correct you and take you to court
> > because of your piety?
> > **5** Isn't your wickedness abundant
> > and aren't your iniquities endless?

Job: The Cry of the Righteous Sufferer

Eliphaz starts out cold and then goes to deep freeze. *What does God need with you? What does even a wise man offer him?* The implication is that God is not impressed with Job's puny protests of innocence. It adds nothing to God if Job straightens up. Job is foolish to act as though his protests of innocence will reach God's ears and somehow procure a hearing before him. It is not because of Job's piety that God is taking him to task, but because of sin, says Eliphaz. We know better. We know it is *expressly* because of Job's piety that all this is happening.

Millions, if not billions, of theists today believe in a God like Eliphaz describes. They see him essentially as standing over a set of heavenly scales, weighing man's deeds but not truly caring for him. To them, God does not fellowship with man, or take pleasure in his piety. He mostly stands around with a large mallet waiting to play whack-a-mole whenever his creatures screw up.

How does God's revelation of Himself in the Bible present a completely different picture, especially in the person of Jesus?

There is no pretense of being subtle in the accusation of v.5. Eliphaz issues the most direct accusation to this point, charging that there is no end to Job's wickedness. *Friends? Have these guys even met?* The only explanation for such a harsh accusation from a good friend is that he sees no other possible reason for Job's current situation. The walls of his theology are impenetrable indeed!

Job's Injustice Upon Others

It's no wonder Eliphaz presents God as unaffected and uncaring, a simple guardian of the scales of justice. For Eliphaz acts exactly like that. He talks like he and Job have no history together, no prior record of his friend's real character that might earn him some benefit of the doubt. The charges get much worse:

> **6** For you took collateral from your brothers without cause,
> stripping off their clothes and leaving them naked.
> **7** You gave no water to the thirsty
> and withheld food from the famished,
> **8** while the land belonged to a powerful man
> and an influential man lived on it.
> **9** You sent widows away empty-handed,
> and the strength of the fatherless was crushed.
> **10** Therefore snares surround you,
> and sudden dread terrifies you,
> **11** or darkness, so you cannot see,
> and a flood of water covers you.

Round Three: Eliphaz V. Job

> **12** Isn't God as high as the heavens?
> And look at the highest stars—how lofty they are!
> **13** Yet you say, "What does God know?
> Can he judge through total darkness?
> **14** Clouds veil him so that he cannot see,
> as he walks on the circle of the sky."

Of what things does Eliphaz directly accuse Job in this section?

All these things of which Eliphaz accuses Job are the kinds of abuse of power that have been rampant throughout history. The might-makes-right acts of injustice perpetrated on the weakest and most vulnerable were the targets of the OT prophets of Israel and Judah. When Jesus hit the scene, he too spoke against these injustices, and he spent his public ministry largely with and ministering to the downtrodden.

These accusations are over-the-top and shocking for a friend who in ch.4 painted Job as one who "strengthened weak hands" (v.3), "steadied the one that was stumbling and braced the knees that were buckling" (v.4). Surely, he must now be using extreme hyperbole to shake Job from his stubborn blindness and especially his arrogance (v.13 here).

Come to Terms with God
Though he has struck a cold, hard slap to the face, Eliphaz now seems to genuinely attempt to woo Job back to the right. He presents an invitation of sorts, to reject the path of the wicked (see Ps 1) and to come to terms with God. He attempts to chase Job off the "ancient path" of the wicked with what may be a reference to the judgment of the worldwide flood:

> **15** Will you continue on the ancient path
> that wicked men have walked?
> **16** They were snatched away before their time,
> and their foundations were washed away by a river.
> **17** They were the ones who said to God, "Leave us alone!"
> and "What can the Almighty do to us?"
> **18** But it was he who filled their houses with good things.
> The counsel of the wicked is far from me!
> **19** The righteous see this and rejoice;
> the innocent mock them, saying,
> **20** "Surely our opponents are destroyed,
> and fire has consumed what they left behind."

Job: The Cry of the Righteous Sufferer

> **21** Come to terms with God and be at peace;
> in this way good will come to you.
> **22** Receive instruction from his mouth,
> and place his sayings in your heart.
> **23** If you return to the Almighty, you will be renewed.
> If you banish injustice from your tent
> **24** and consign your gold to the dust,
> the gold of Ophir to the stones in the wadis,
> **25** the Almighty will be your gold
> and your finest silver.
> **26** Then you will delight in the Almighty
> and lift up your face to God.
> **27** You will pray to him, and he will hear you,
> and you will fulfill your vows.
> **28** When you make a decision, it will be carried out,
> and light will shine on your ways.
> **29** When others are humiliated and you say, "Lift them up,"
> God will save the humble.
> **30** He will even rescue the guilty one,
> who will be rescued by the purity of your hands.

Even if Eliphaz is trying to persuade, there is still a lot of bite in this section. In v.18, he all but quotes Job's words from 21:16: "But their prosperity is not of their own doing. The counsel of the wicked is far from me!" He seems to imply that Job was not in the position to assert such truth, but Eliphaz is.

The friend's invitation, if heeded, will bring "renewal" (v.23). "Com[ing] to terms" and "peace" (v.21) are often used as military terms (Dt 20:12; Josh 10:1,4; 11:19; 2 Sam 10:19; 1 Chr 19:19), here indicating a surrender on Job's part to reconcile with God. Notice the terms of prosperity that are voiced in vv.25-30. Eliphaz at least uses material wealth to point to spiritual wealth (vv.24-25) but notice again the one-sided nature of the God-man relationship. Job will delight in God (v.26), but there is no hint that God will delight in him. What a sadly lacking view! Notice once again that the dogmatic language of vv.27-30 seems to put man in the driver's seat.

Eliphaz's invitation to shun the path of the wicked and to instead pursue the way of God is ironic. Of course, it is good advice! It sounds like the wisdom of Psalm 1. It is much like the invitation of Josh 24:14-15: "Choose for yourselves today: Which [god] will you worship? As for me and my family, we will worship the LORD." It is ironic here for Job because he has done exactly that, and his fidelity to God is exactly why Job is in this mess. In this case, the invitation is most insulting.

How does Job's situation illustrate the importance of the Christian to be Spirit-led and discerning to speak the right truth at the right time?

Round Three: Eliphaz V. Job

Have you ever sensed the Holy Spirit directing – or redirecting – what you spoke into a situation or how you acted? How did you respond, and how did it turn out?

Job's Reply

If Only...
Perhaps Job is getting too weary to strike back, or maybe he sees it as futile. He does not parry with a personal retort this time. He simply responds with a bit of a wish list in what seems to be a soliloquy, a speech not really directed at his friend(s) or at God:

> **Job 23**
> **1** Then Job answered:
>
> > **2** Today also my complaint is bitter.
> > His hand is heavy despite my groaning.
> > **3** If only I knew how to find him,
> > so that I could go to his throne.
> > **4** I would plead my case before him
> > and fill my mouth with arguments.
> > **5** I would learn how he would answer me;
> > and understand what he would say to me.
> > **6** Would he prosecute me forcefully?
> > No, he would certainly pay attention to me.
> > **7** Then an upright man could reason with him,
> > and I would escape from my Judge forever.

Notice how Job's statements fly in the face of the caricatures his friends paint of him. They accuse him of the height of arrogance, but here he seeks to plead with God, not charge him (v.4). He would learn of him and seek understanding (v.5). Because Job knows himself to be properly humble in these things, he is confident that his Judge would pay attention to him and reason with him, rather than "forcefully prosecuting" him (v.6). Job seems aware that God "resists the proud but gives grace to the humble" (1 Pt 5:5).

If only...

How does Job in this section express more cravings that are answered by the gospel?

Job: The Cry of the Righteous Sufferer

I Cannot Perceive Him
Job goes on to let all the air out of his "if only" balloon:

> **8** If I go east, he is not there,
> and if I go west, I cannot perceive him.
> **9** When he is at work to the north, I cannot see him;
> when he turns south, I cannot find him.

When you have you felt like God was either "not there" or was at least imperceptible? What did you do?

Yet He Knows
Even in this moment of divine disconnect, Job has a core confidence. This is the stuff his friends cannot access. He knows he has remained true to God in his will and his way:

> **10** Yet he knows the way I have taken;
> when he has tested me, I will emerge as pure gold.
> **11** My feet have followed in his tracks;
> I have kept to his way and not turned aside.
> **12** I have not departed from the commands from his lips;
> I have treasured the words from his mouth
> more than my daily food.

The picture of Job "emerging as gold" is one of revelation rather than purification. Testing may function in either way, to purify or to reveal as pure, or perhaps a mixture of both. Job's emphasis here is that his testing will reveal his purity. This also agrees with the theme of the whole book, that Job's purity – or integrity – will be vindicated by God before the *satan*, before Job's friends and before every reader of this text.

What reasons does Job give for his confidence?

How does the phrase, "when he has tested me" relate to this whole book?

Round Three: Eliphaz V. Job

How does the NT affirm that testing is an essential part of a Christian's life?

Compare Job's statement with the psalmist:

> **Psalm 119:102–103**
> **102** I have not turned from your judgments,
> for you yourself have instructed me.
> **103** How sweet your word is to my taste—
> sweeter than honey in my mouth.

While we cannot be sure of the manner by which Job had access to God's word, we can be sure that his response was the same as the psalmist's. Job followed God's commands and his way. The word translated "tracks" in v.11 is a beautiful picture. The term "way" refers to one's *manner of life*, while "tracks" is more concrete, and might be translated "path" (NASB) or "steps" (ESV, NIV, NRSV, NET). The picture is that Job is following the steps of God himself, steps that have been blazed into a trail by the wise who have also followed these steps before Job.

What He Has Decreed for Me

Job's commitment to God's path causes him mixed emotions. Job expresses both confidence and faintheartedness:

> **13** But he is unchangeable; who can oppose him?
> He does what he desires.
> **14** He will certainly accomplish what he has decreed for me,
> and he has many more things like these in mind.
> **15** Therefore I am terrified in his presence;
> when I consider this, I am afraid of him.
> **16** God has made my heart faint;
> the Almighty has terrified me.
> **17** Yet I am not destroyed by the darkness,
> by the thick darkness that covers my face.

In what ways does Job express confidence here, and in what or whom?

What seems to terrify Job, and why?

Job: The Cry of the Righteous Sufferer

So, Job has several reasons for confidence. First, he is humble before God, and that leads him to expect grace. Second, he knows he has faithfully followed God's way and his commands. Third, he knows God will surely accomplish everything he has in mind for Job (which he nervously hopes will once again turn out to be *good* things). Last, even though God's presence is terrifying, it is still a security against "the darkness" (v.17).

Do these reasons for confidence resonate with you? If so, how?

Why?

Job has bemoaned the fact that he cannot find an audience with God. He has expressed the reasons for his confidence were God to come reason with him. He has also acknowledged that this turn of events in God's "wonderful plan for his life" makes him really nervous about what else God has in store for him. Now Job falls back to his questioning of the injustices in the world, wondering why on earth God allows the wicked to sin openly, to oppress and abuse, to prey on and destroy the helpless:

Job 24

> 1 Why does the Almighty not reserve times for judgment?
> Why do those who know him never see his days?
> 2 The wicked displace boundary markers.
> They steal a flock and provide pasture for it.
> 3 They drive away the donkeys owned by the fatherless
> and take the widow's ox as collateral.
> 4 They push the needy off the road;
> the poor of the land are forced into hiding.
> 5 Like wild donkeys in the wilderness,
> the poor go out to their task of foraging for food;
> the desert provides nourishment for their children.
> 6 They gather their fodder in the field
> and glean the vineyards of the wicked.
> 7 Without clothing, they spend the night naked,
> having no covering against the cold.
> 8 Drenched by mountain rains,
> they huddle against the rocks, shelterless.
> 9 The fatherless infant is snatched from the breast;
> the nursing child of the poor is seized as collateral.
> 10 Without clothing, they wander about naked.
> They carry sheaves but go hungry.

Round Three: Eliphaz V. Job

11 They crush olives in their presses;
they tread the winepresses, but go thirsty.
12 From the city, men groan;
the mortally wounded cry for help,
yet God pays no attention to this crime.
13 The wicked are those who rebel against the light.
They do not recognize its ways
or stay on its paths.
14 The murderer rises at dawn
to kill the poor and needy,
and by night he becomes a thief.
15 The adulterer's eye watches for twilight,
thinking, "No eye will see me,"
and he covers his face.
16 In the dark they break into houses;
by day they lock themselves in,
never experiencing the light.
17 For the morning is like darkness to them.
Surely they are familiar with the terrors of darkness!

How do deeds of the wicked listed here intensify as Job progresses?

What kind of evil deeds are performed in the dark of night in vv.13-17? How does literal darkness represent spiritual darkness?

The next section gives many interpreters pause. Some argue these words are not Job's. It sounds more like Job's friends to say that the wicked are thwarted by God. Still, just as Job has expressed both confidence and terror in God, it may well be that he can voice two apparent contradictions here about God and the wicked.

Job has just given eyewitness account of God's apparent inactivity in stopping evil men from their wicked deeds, and now he explains that God does in fact seem to oppose the wicked in this life. We have noticed all along that Job does not disagree with his friends that God is against the wicked. He has simply pointed out that many times it seems that God is forestalling his judgment for some later time. Job's point is that absolute statements to either extreme (God always brings retribution or he never does) do not seem to draw in the full scope of God's justice. Though God does seem to let much evil slide by, it is also true that he does bring evil back on the heads of those who perpetrate it:

> 18 They float on the surface of the water.
> Their section of the land is cursed,
> so that they never go to their vineyards.
> 19 As dry ground and heat snatch away the melted snow,
> so Sheol steals those who have sinned.
> 20 The womb forgets them;
> worms feed on them;
> they are remembered no more.
> So injustice is broken like a tree.
> 21 They prey on the childless woman who is unable to conceive,
> and do not deal kindly with the widow.
> 22 Yet God drags away the mighty by his power;
> when he rises up, they have no assurance of life.
> 23 He gives them a sense of security, so they can rely on it,
> but his eyes watch over their ways.
> 24 They are exalted for a moment, then gone;
> they are brought low and shrivel up like everything else.
> They wither like heads of grain.
> 25 If this is not true, then who can prove me a liar
> and show that my speech is worthless?

Assuming it is indeed Job speaking here, the difference is that when his friends made such assertions about the wicked, they were directing them at Job as though he was lumped in with them. Job is speaking about the wicked from his perspective as a righteous man.

Reflection on Testing as Proving
How have you observed that testing in this life reveals much of what is true about someone's character and way as either righteous or wicked?

What have you seen that tells you that this life cannot adequately account for justice for either the righteous or the wicked, that there must be a final judgment?

Lesson 12 Dialogue: Round Three: Bildad V. Job (Chs.25 - 27)

Bildad's Last Brief Barrage

Out of Blows

We have observed that Job's friends have not really been introducing new substance for their conclusions in Rounds Two and Three. Rather than proving false Job's claims of innocence (which they cannot do), they have simply appropriated Job's suffering as the single and – they think – overwhelming evidence of his guilt. They have *assumed* wickedness must be in Job's heart and attitude, since they cannot *prove* it so.

Worse, along with their presumption of Job's guilt, they have then extrapolated trumped up charges that Job has committed injustices against his fellow man, especially the weak and helpless. There is no way they could prove Job guilty of inward corruption and neither is there any evidence that he has acted wickedly toward others. These accusations contradict the friends' own statements at the beginning of the dialogue.

So, it seems with nothing new to offer, the friends' collective case is all but exhausted. The men have tag-teamed in their bout with Job. Zophar won't even offer a third try. And now, like an exhausted heavyweight, Bildad musters one last one-two combination that carries minimal momentum and has little chance of landing a knock-out.

Power and Purity

> **Job 25**
> **1** Then Bildad the Shuhite replied:
> **2** Dominion and dread belong to him,
> the one who establishes harmony in his heights.
> **3** Can his troops be numbered?
> Does his light not shine on everyone?
> **4** How can a human be justified before God?
> How can one born of woman be pure?
> **5** If even the moon does not shine
> and the stars are not pure in his sight,
> **6** how much less a human, who is a maggot,
> a son of man, who is a worm!

Even in these six verses, Bildad borrows from what has already been said. Eliphaz and Job already voiced the questions from v.4. Eliphaz in 4:17 and again in 15:14 had already asked how a mere human could be pure before God. Job himself had already agreed with Bildad's point in 9:2, when he asked first, "How can a person be justified before God?"

Job: The Cry of the Righteous Sufferer

If Bildad introduces anything new, it is the concept of "dominion" in v.2, but the reality of God's unchallenged and dreadful sovereign power has been a common theme. Here it is presented with the particular nuance of a kingdom and the military might (v.3) to dominate. Bildad asserts that God maintains his unchallenged rule ("harmony" in v.2 indicates the peace that is opposite of war). This rule is maintained in and from the heavens ("heights") to and upon the earth and encompasses "everyone" (v.3).

Bildad emphasizes not only God's power but also his purity, as we have already observed. Bildad presents this truth from the greater to the lesser. If celestial objects (or beings), which are nearer to God, cannot measure up to God's purity, then man even less so. Bildad borrows from Eliphaz again (4:18; 15:15) as well as Job (21:22).

As we have seen throughout these interchanges, Bildad is speaking the truth once again. Of course, Job would not and does not disagree with these statements. In fact, we might wonder why Bildad even bothered to assemble these words into his last flurry. There is no rebuke, no call to repent, not even any apparent implications regarding Job. Just bare theological facts.

From this doctrinal standpoint, it is worth noting where some other biblical writers have used the language of v.6 to refer to mankind's unique relationship to God:

> **Psalm 8:3–8**
> **3** When I observe your heavens,
> the work of your fingers,
> the moon and the stars,
> which you set in place,
> **4** what is a human being that you remember him,
> a son of man that you look after him?
> **5** You made him little less than God
> and crowned him with glory and honor.
> **6** You made him ruler over the works of your hands;
> you put everything under his feet:
> **7** all the sheep and oxen,
> as well as the animals in the wild,
> **8** the birds of the sky,
> and the fish of the sea
> that pass through the currents of the seas.
>
> **Psalm 22:1–8**
> **1** My God, my God, why have you abandoned me?
> Why are you so far from my deliverance
> and from my words of groaning?

Round Three: Bildad V. Job

2 My God, I cry by day, but you do not answer,
by night, yet I have no rest.
3 But you are holy,
enthroned on the praises of Israel.
4 Our ancestors trusted in you;
they trusted, and you rescued them.
5 They cried to you and were set free;
they trusted in you and were not disgraced.
6 But I am a worm and not a man,
scorned by mankind and despised by people.
7 Everyone who sees me mocks me;
they sneer and shake their heads:
8 "He relies on the Lord;
let him save him;
let the Lord rescue him,
since he takes pleasure in him."

Isaiah 41:11–14
11 Be sure that all who are enraged against you
will be ashamed and disgraced;
those who contend with you
will become as nothing and will perish.
12 You will look for those who contend with you,
but you will not find them.
Those who war against you
will become absolutely nothing.
13 For I am the Lord your God,
who holds your right hand,
who says to you, "Do not fear,
I will help you.
14 Do not fear, you worm Jacob,
you men of Israel.
I will help you"—
this is the Lord's declaration.
Your Redeemer is the Holy One of Israel.

How do these passages cooperate with Bildad's point to show that man is far beneath God?

Job: The Cry of the Righteous Sufferer

How do they also speak to the opposite truth, that God has given man privileged status?

How do both these truths relate to Job's situation and his arguments?

Job's "Haymaker"

Back Atcha (Sarcasm Again)
If Bildad's last swings were into thin air, Job lands a parting shot squarely on the jaw. From whom have these remarks come, these reminders that Job is a mere human? From a human! Bildad's insights are not news to Job, and what's more, they are no help:

> **Job 26**
> **1** Then Job answered:
> **2** How you have helped the powerless
> and delivered the arm that is weak!
> **3** How you have counseled the unwise
> and abundantly provided insight!
> **4** With whom did you speak these words?
> Whose breath came out of your mouth?

Whispers of God's Greatness
Job will take Bildad's comments further. God is so awesome in his power that man has only heard faint whispers of his true magnificence:

> **5** The departed spirits tremble
> beneath the waters and all that inhabit them.
> **6** Sheol is naked before God,
> and Abaddon has no covering.
> **7** He stretches the northern skies over empty space;
> he hangs the earth on nothing.
> **8** He wraps up the water in his clouds,
> yet the clouds do not burst beneath its weight.
> **9** He obscures the view of his throne,
> spreading his cloud over it.

Round Three: Bildad V. Job

> **10** He laid out the horizon on the surface of the waters
> at the boundary between light and darkness.
> **11** The pillars that hold up the sky tremble,
> astounded at his rebuke.
> **12** By his power he stirred the sea,
> and by his understanding he crushed Rahab.
> **13** By his breath the heavens gained their beauty;
> his hand pierced the fleeing serpent.
> **14** These are but the fringes of his ways;
> how faint is the word we hear of him!
> Who can understand his mighty thunder?

God's dominion extends to the grave, to Sheol itself (vv.5-6). He is the utterly transcendent Creator who established and sustains the cosmos (vv.7-13). He subdues the chaos of the sea and subdues its monsters as well (Rahab is a reference to such a monster, cf., Is 51:9). God has created the beauty of the heavens (v.13) but obscures his far greater glory behind the clouds where his throne is (v.9).

What reason does Job give for why the "departed spirits tremble" and what does this imply about God's sovereign judgment?

Job's Oath

Upon affirming God's total dominance as the Creator, Job has established the highest possible standard upon which to stake his innocence. He could hardly use stronger language to affirm his innocence and to state his resolve. After all the talk, this is Job's heaviest swing, his haymaker:

> **Job 27**
> **1** Job continued his discourse, saying:
> **2** As God lives, who has deprived me of justice,
> and the Almighty who has made me bitter,
> **3** as long as my breath is still in me
> and the breath from God remains in my nostrils,
> **4** my lips will not speak unjustly,
> and my tongue will not utter deceit.
> **5** I will never affirm that you are right.
> I will maintain my integrity until I die.
> **6** I will cling to my righteousness and never let it go.
> My conscience will not accuse me as long as I live!

Job: The Cry of the Righteous Sufferer

Here Job gives somewhat of a summary statement. He still holds that this calamity has come from God, though he is undeserving (v.2). Still, he acknowledges God's sustaining grace in his life (v.3) and resolves to speak the truth (v.4). He stubbornly defends himself against the charges of his friends (v.5), and then summarizes all his arguments in declaring that his conscience is clear. All these remarks are prefaced with and subject to a sort of oath: "As God lives..." This statement is akin to swearing "on a stack of Bibles" in our modern culture. There was no more iron-clad witness available than that of the Almighty God.

Have you ever been desperate to be believed, ready to use the strongest language like this?

How are Job's statements here tied all the way back to the prologue?

Job's Curse

From his firm resolutions before God about his own innocence and commitment to integrity, Job turns to his fellow man. We are familiar with various forms of blessings. For example, "May the road always rise up to meet you," or "May the wind be always at your back." Here, Job uses the formula the opposite way to pronounce a curse upon his enemy:

> **7** May my enemy be like the wicked
> and my opponent like the unjust.
> **8** For what hope does the godless person have when he is cut off,
> when God takes away his life?
> **9** Will God hear his cry
> when distress comes on him?
> **10** Will he delight in the Almighty?
> Will he call on God at all times?
> **11** I will teach you about God's power.
> I will not conceal what the Almighty has planned.
> **12** All of you have seen this for yourselves,
> why do you keep up this empty talk?

To whom do you suppose Job is referring with "enemy" and "opponent" in v.7?

Round Three: Bildad V. Job

Who was Job's true enemy of which he was not aware?

How is this a powerful reminder for us when discerning our opposition?

More than one commentator points out that Job has repeatedly called upon God (v.10) while it is not recorded once that any of his friends do. This stark contrast points out that Job is not the one who has behaved like the godless person.

Under the law given to Moses, if someone was falsely accused in court, those bringing the false charges were subject to the punishments fitting the crime of the accused. Much like that here, Job throws the threat of punishment back on his false accusers. The friends have set themselves up for a complete reversal of their pronouncements of judgment upon Job. But for God's grace – and Job's intercession – they themselves would be liable to experience this reversal in the conclusion of this story.

All the pronouns in vv.11-12 are plural, and clearly indicate that Job is collecting all three friends in his last rebuke. Job essentially says, "Now let me teach YOU all a thing or two!"

The Wicked Man's Lot
To drive the point home further, Job takes up a familiar sounding speech declaring the fate of the wicked man. His friends have used such dramatic poetry to rebuke and warn him, but now Job throws it back upon their own heads:

> **13** This is a wicked man's lot from God,
> the inheritance the ruthless receive from the Almighty.
> **14** Even if his children increase, they are destined for the sword;
> his descendants will never have enough food.
> **15** Those who survive him will be buried by the plague,
> yet their widows will not weep for them.
> **16** Though he piles up silver like dust
> and heaps up fine clothing like clay—
> **17** he may heap it up, but the righteous will wear it,
> and the innocent will divide up his silver.
> **18** The house he built is like a moth's cocoon
> or a shelter set up by a watchman.

19 He lies down wealthy, but will do so no more;
when he opens his eyes, it is gone.
20 Terrors overtake him like a flood;
a storm wind sweeps him away at night.
21 An east wind picks him up, and he is gone;
it carries him away from his place.
22 It blasts at him without mercy,
while he flees desperately from its force.
23 It claps its hands at him
and scoffs at him from its place.

What words or phrases above sound familiar from the rebukes of Job's friends?

Since the descriptions of the wicked man's lot are very similar to what the friends have described, how are they different coming from Job's lips?

Gospel Realities

How does being "naked before God" (26:6) anticipate the need for a Savior in the final judgment?

How does God's "hand pierc[ing] the fleeing serpent" (v.13 with Is 27:1; Rv 13:1; 20:2,10) foreshadow Christ's victory over Satan?

How do "delight[ing] in God" and "call[ing] upon him at all times" (Jb 27:10) describe the life of faith and worship that is expressed today in following Christ?

Round Three: Bildad V. Job

How does "maintain[ing] my integrity until I die" (v.5) anticipate the perseverance of the saints (cf. Php 1:6; 1 Cor 10:13)?

Lesson 13 Dialogue: Job's Hymn to Wisdom and Closing Statement (Chs.28 - 31)

Job has withstood the accusations of his friends. He has asserted that he has retained his integrity, and he has vowed to maintain it to his death. Further, he has cursed his enemies who will not call out to God like he does. While he has argued that much in life does not seem to go according to God's perfect justice, he knows that ultimately it will. He cannot make sense of his own terrible situation, but he knows God is perfectly trustworthy. Even with all his questions, Job knows the destruction of the wicked is final. He hopes that somehow things will turn better for him.

Job pivots. He has been defending himself against his friends. They read his situation, and because of all his troubles they lump him in with the wicked. He has argued it is not so. He actually agrees with their statements that the wicked will suffer judgment, though by human reckoning it doesn't always seem to come soon enough. Now Job turns to the foundational principle that drives and guides the righteous. He delivers a soliloquy on *wisdom*, proclaiming its value, much like what we find in Prv 2. Wisdom is a hidden treasure.

Hymn to Wisdom

The Miner and Earthly Treasures
First, Job gives the picture of earthly treasures and those who search and work for them:

> **Job 28**
> **1** Surely there is a mine for silver
> and a place where gold is refined.
> **2** Iron is taken from the ground,
> and copper is smelted from ore.
> **3** A miner puts an end to the darkness;
> he probes the deepest recesses
> for ore in the gloomy darkness.
> **4** He cuts a shaft far from human habitation,
> in places unknown to those who walk above ground.
> Suspended far away from people,
> the miners swing back and forth.
> **5** Food may come from the earth,
> but below the surface the earth is transformed as by fire.
> **6** Its rocks are a source of lapis lazuli,
> containing flecks of gold.
> **7** No bird of prey knows that path;
> no falcon's eye has seen it.

Job: The Cry of the Righteous Sufferer

> **8** Proud beasts have never walked on it;
> no lion has ever prowled over it.
> **9** The miner uses a flint tool
> and turns up ore from the root of the mountains.
> **10** He cuts out channels in the rocks,
> and his eyes spot every treasure.
> **11** He dams up the streams from flowing
> so that he may bring to light what is hidden.

How does Job describe the hiddenness of earthly treasures?

What words describe the work of the miner to obtain these treasures?

Job says that fire transforms the earth to create treasures (v.5). The miner works to reveal them (v.11). These ideas are a metaphor for the work of suffering that God uses to reveal treasures of integrity in those he has made from the earth. Through suffering God refines (v.1), smelts (v.2) and works on a person (vv.9-10) to "bring to light what is hidden" (v.11).

The Value and Elusiveness of Wisdom
Job moves from the literal to the figurative. We have mines for gold, silver, and precious stones, but where does one find a mine for wisdom?

> **12** But where can wisdom be found,
> and where is understanding located?
> **13** No one can know its value,
> since it cannot be found in the land of the living.
> **14** The ocean depths say, "It's not in me,"
> while the sea declares, "I don't have it."
> **15** Gold cannot be exchanged for it,
> and silver cannot be weighed out for its price.
> **16** Wisdom cannot be valued in the gold of Ophir,
> in precious onyx or lapis lazuli.
> **17** Gold and glass do not compare with it,
> and articles of fine gold cannot be exchanged for it.

Job's Hymn to Wisdom and Closing Statement

18 Coral and quartz are not worth mentioning.
The price of wisdom is beyond pearls.
19 Topaz from Cush cannot compare with it,
and it cannot be valued in pure gold.
20 Where then does wisdom come from,
and where is understanding located?
21 It is hidden from the eyes of every living thing
and concealed from the birds of the sky.
22 Abaddon and Death say,
"We have heard news of it with our ears."

What possible search areas for "wisdom mines" are ruled OUT in 13-14 and 21-22? How would you summarize, and where does that leave the treasure hunter to explore?

Since Abaddon and Death speak of the grave or the underworld, what do you make of their response to the treasure hunter seeking wisdom?

The Source for Wisdom

Treasure hunters have been around for all human history. The myth of Midas tells us that there is one thing better than finding treasure. If you have the power to create it your wealth is infinite. Job argues from the lesser to the greater that God knows where the treasure of wisdom is. Far greater than that, he is the one who established it:

23 But God understands the way to wisdom,
and he knows its location.
24 For he looks to the ends of the earth
and sees everything under the heavens.
25 When God fixed the weight of the wind
and distributed the water by measure,
26 when he established a limit for the rain
and a path for the lightning,
27 he considered wisdom and evaluated it;
he established it and examined it.

> **28** He said to mankind,
> "The fear of the Lord—that is wisdom.
> And to turn from evil is understanding."

God doesn't just *understand* wisdom, he is wisdom's *source*. If wisdom were gold, God would be King Midas. Wisdom flows from his all-knowing mind and is expressed in his all-powerful actions to create and sustain, from the beginning of creation and forevermore. What is most important to us is that God has revealed wisdom to *us*. He has done this in the self-evident ways of the universe. Theologians call that General Revelation. Paul argues this point in Rm 1. But God has revealed himself and his wisdom in much more refined ways through his Word and his Son. We call that Special Revelation.

For these reasons, Job gives God's own summary of what wisdom is for man. It is to fear the Lord and to turn from evil (v.28). This is essentially the same definition God inspires the Teacher of Ecclesiastes to give: "When all has been heard, the conclusion of the matter is this: fear God and keep his commands, because this is for all humanity" (Ec 12:13).

How does God's definition of wisdom in Jb 28:28 compare with the definition of (Job's) integrity in 1:1,8 and 2:3?

How is that significant, especially since Job is the one saying it in 28:28?

Job's Closing Statement

The Good Ol' Days
God's definition corresponds exactly to the descriptions of Job's way of life. Now, Job begins to reflect on that life. First, he reminisces about the good old days when God's blessings were abundant:

> **Job 29**
> **1** Job continued his discourse, saying:
> **2** If only I could be as in months gone by,
> in the days when God watched over me,
> **3** when his lamp shone above my head,
> and I walked through darkness by his light!

Job's Hymn to Wisdom and Closing Statement

4 I would be as I was in the days of my youth
when God's friendship rested on my tent,
5 when the Almighty was still with me
and my children were around me,
6 when my feet were bathed in curds
and the rock poured out streams of oil for me!
7 When I went out to the city gate
and took my seat in the town square,
8 the young men saw me and withdrew,
while older men stood to their feet.
9 City officials stopped talking
and covered their mouths with their hands.
10 The noblemen's voices were hushed,
and their tongues stuck to the roof of their mouths.
11 When they heard me, they blessed me,
and when they saw me, they spoke well of me.
12 For I rescued the poor who cried out for help,
and the fatherless child who had no one to support him.
13 The dying blessed me,
and I made the widow's heart rejoice.
14 I clothed myself in righteousness,
and it enveloped me;
my just decisions were like a robe and a turban.
15 I was eyes to the blind
and feet to the lame.
16 I was a father to the needy,
and I examined the case of the stranger.
17 I shattered the fangs of the unjust
and snatched the prey from his teeth.
18 So I thought, "I will die in my own nest
and multiply my days as the sand.
19 My roots will have access to water,
and the dew will rest on my branches all night.
20 My whole being will be refreshed within me,
and my bow will be renewed in my hand."
21 Men listened to me with expectation,
waiting silently for my advice.
22 After a word from me they did not speak again;
my speech settled on them like dew.
23 They waited for me as for the rain
and opened their mouths as for spring showers.

Job: The Cry of the Righteous Sufferer

> 24 If I smiled at them, they couldn't believe it;
> they were thrilled at the light of my countenance.
> 25 I directed their course and presided as chief.
> I lived as a king among his troops,
> like one who comforts those who mourn.

How were the good ol' days for Job himself?

How did they affect his family?

How did they impact his community?

What does this speech remind us about the impact of our own experiences today?

These Days of Suffering
The good ol' days are gone. Job takes a turn from "If only…" to "But now…"

> **Job 30**
> 1 But now they mock me,
> men younger than I am,
> whose fathers I would have refused to put
> with my sheep dogs.
> 2 What use to me was the strength of their hands?
> Their vigor had left them.
> 3 Emaciated from poverty and hunger,
> they gnawed the dry land,
> the desolate wasteland by night.
> 4 They plucked mallow among the shrubs,
> and the roots of the broom tree were their food.

Job's Hymn to Wisdom and Closing Statement

5 They were banished from human society;
people shouted at them as if they were thieves.
6 They are living on the slopes of the wadis,
among the rocks and in holes in the ground.
7 They bray among the shrubs;
they huddle beneath the thistles.
8 Foolish men, without even a name.
They were forced to leave the land.
9 Now I am mocked by their songs;
I have become an object of scorn to them.
10 They despise me and keep their distance from me;
they do not hesitate to spit in my face.
11 Because God has loosened my bowstring and oppressed me,
they have cast off restraint in my presence.
12 The rabble rise up at my right;
they trap my feet
and construct their siege ramp against me.
13 They tear up my path;
they contribute to my destruction,
without anyone to help them.
14 They advance as through a gaping breach;
they keep rolling in through the ruins.
15 Terrors are turned loose against me;
they chase my dignity away like the wind,
and my prosperity has passed by like a cloud.
16 Now my life is poured out before me,
and days of suffering have seized me.
17 Night pierces my bones,
but my gnawing pains never rest.
18 My clothing is distorted with great force;
he chokes me by the neck of my garment.
19 He throws me into the mud,
and I have become like dust and ashes.
20 I cry out to you for help, but you do not answer me;
when I stand up, you merely look at me.
21 You have turned against me with cruelty;
you harass me with your strong hand.
22 You lift me up on the wind and make me ride it;
you scatter me in the storm.
23 Yes, I know that you will lead me to death—
the place appointed for all who live.

Job: The Cry of the Righteous Sufferer

24 Yet no one would stretch out his hand
against a ruined person
when he cries out to him for help
because of his distress.
25 Have I not wept for those who have fallen on hard times?
Has my soul not grieved for the needy?
26 But when I hoped for good, evil came;
when I looked for light, darkness came.
27 I am churning within and cannot rest;
days of suffering confront me.
28 I walk about blackened, but not by the sun.
I stood in the assembly and cried out for help.
29 I have become a brother to jackals
and a companion of ostriches.
30 My skin blackens and flakes off,
and my bones burn with fever.
31 My lyre is used for mourning
and my flute for the sound of weeping.

How do these descriptions show a complete reversal for Job?

Once again, from whose hand does Job see all this as coming?

Job used to sense God's presence and blessing. He was watched over and enlightened (29:2-3). God was with him, like a close friend of the family (vv.5-6). Job was not only blessed by God but blessed and revered by his community (vv.7-11). And rightfully so! Job was a pillar of his community, one who helped the helpless and promoted justice (vv.12-17). He was a godly advocate, advisor, judge, and even ruler (vv.21-25). In short, the descriptions of him by the writer and by God himself in chs.1-2 were also how Job perceived himself. He knew he had feared God and turned away from evil. He also knew he had not turned from this path of integrity, and he declared he never would.

For all those reasons, Job expected his blessing and comfort to continue throughout his life (29:18-22). His reasoning was like his friends' reasoning. Why would God pull the rug out from under him when he was being faithful?

Job's Hymn to Wisdom and Closing Statement

But that upsetting turn came in a scope Job would never have imagined. As we saw in Lesson 4, it may well be that deep down Job feared this could happen, but in his day-to-day life it seemed virtually impossible. Still, it had happened.

The worthless outcast now mocks and attacks him (30:1-15). He who advocated for the weak is downtrodden most of all. Add to that the fact that his body is riddled with pain and suffering (vv.16-19). Where is his help, his advocate? He has none. Even God, who had blessed him and been as a dear friend, even he does not answer (vv.20-23). There is no one to help as Job would have (vv.24-26). We know this includes his three friends, and it is because they choose to judge rather than comfort him (12:5). He has been burned black, and it is not sunburn (vv.28-30). It is the fires of testing and adversity and suffering. And he endures it alone, an outcast like a jackal or an ostrich, abandoned – he feels – by his community, his friends, even his wife, and worst of all, by God. The celebration song of his life has turned to a dirge (v.31).

Have you ever been enjoying a good day or season in life, and been a little paranoid, wondering when the storm would hit? If so, why do you suppose this is?

Consider these two passages by the Teacher of wisdom in Ecclesiastes:

Ecclesiastes 3:13–14
13 It is also the gift of God whenever anyone eats, drinks, and enjoys all his efforts. **14** I know that everything God does will last forever; there is no adding to it or taking from it. God works so that people will be in awe of him.

Ecclesiastes 5:18–20
18 Here is what I have seen to be good: It is appropriate to eat, drink, and experience good in all the labor one does under the sun during the few days of his life God has given him, because that is his reward. **19** Furthermore, everyone to whom God has given riches and wealth, he has also allowed him to enjoy them, take his reward, and rejoice in his labor. This is a gift of God, **20** for he does not often consider the days of his life because God keeps him occupied with the joy of his heart.

Why and how should good times in this life be enjoyed?

What is the only kind of joy that lasts forever?

Job: The Cry of the Righteous Sufferer

How can we find balance in enjoying fleeting good times now, and what hope for joy can we have when things fall apart?

One Last Protest of Innocence

Job now issues a summary statement, like a defense attorney covering every possible angle for a jury before resting his case. With a series of "if-then" scenarios Job surveys the major common categories for human wickedness. *If I am guilty of any of these, Your Honor, then convict and give sentence. But if the crime does not fit, "you must acquit!"*

Lust:

> **Job 31**
> **1** I have made a covenant with my eyes.
> How then could I look at a young woman?
> **2** For what portion would I have from God above,
> or what inheritance from the Almighty on high?
> **3** Doesn't disaster come to the unjust
> and misfortune to evildoers?
> **4** Does he not see my ways
> and number all my steps?

Lying:

> **5** If I have walked in falsehood
> or my foot has rushed to deceit,
> **6** let God weigh me on accurate scales,
> and he will recognize my integrity.

Rebellion/Impurity:

> **7** If my step has turned from the way,
> my heart has followed my eyes,
> or impurity has stained my hands,
> **8** let someone else eat what I have sown,
> and let my crops be uprooted.

Covetousness/Adultery:

> **9** If my heart has gone astray over a woman
> or I have lurked at my neighbor's door,
> **10** let my own wife grind grain for another man,
> and let other men sleep with her.

Job's Hymn to Wisdom and Closing Statement

11 For that would be a disgrace;
it would be an iniquity deserving punishment.
12 For it is a fire that consumes down to Abaddon;
it would destroy my entire harvest.

Injustice/Abuse

13 If I have dismissed the case of my male or female servants
when they made a complaint against me,
14 what could I do when God stands up to judge?
How should I answer him when he calls me to account?
15 Did not the one who made me in the womb also make them?
Did not the same God form us both in the womb?

Neglect

16 If I have refused the wishes of the poor
or let the widow's eyes go blind,
17 if I have eaten my few crumbs alone
without letting the fatherless eat any of it—
18 for from my youth, I raised him as his father,
and since the day I was born I guided the widow—
19 if I have seen anyone dying for lack of clothing
or a needy person without a cloak,
20 if he did not bless me
while warming himself with the fleece from my sheep,
21 if I ever cast my vote against a fatherless child
when I saw that I had support in the city gate,
22 then let my shoulder blade fall from my back,
and my arm be pulled from its socket.
23 For disaster from God terrifies me,
and because of his majesty I could not do these things.

Greed/Idolatry

24 If I placed my confidence in gold
or called fine gold my trust,
25 if I have rejoiced because my wealth is great
or because my own hand has acquired so much,
26 if I have gazed at the sun when it was shining
or at the moon moving in splendor,
27 so that my heart was secretly enticed
and I threw them a kiss,

Job: The Cry of the Righteous Sufferer

   28 this would also be an iniquity deserving punishment,
   for I would have denied God above.

Hate/Vengeance

   29 Have I rejoiced over my enemy's distress,
   or become excited when trouble came his way?
   30 I have not allowed my mouth to sin
   by asking for his life with a curse.

Selfishness

   31 Haven't the members of my household said,
   "Who is there who has not had enough to eat at Job's table?"
   32 No stranger had to spend the night on the street,
   for I opened my door to the traveler.

Pride

   33 Have I covered my transgressions as others do
   by hiding my iniquity in my heart
   34 because I greatly feared the crowds
   and because the contempt of the clans terrified me,
   so I grew silent and would not go outside?

Any Offense

   35 If only I had someone to hear my case!
   Here is my signature; let the Almighty answer me.
   Let my Opponent compose his indictment.
   36 I would surely carry it on my shoulder
   and wear it like a crown.
   37 I would give him an account of all my steps;
   I would approach him like a prince.

Theft

   38 If my land cries out against me
   and its furrows join in weeping,
   39 if I have consumed its produce without payment
   or shown contempt for its tenants,
   40 then let thorns grow instead of wheat
   and stinkweed instead of barley.
   The words of Job are concluded.

Confident of his case, Job voices his problem: he can't find a righteous judge to hear it! His friends have acted like judges, to be sure, but they won't hear the evidence. They are more like the 21st

Job's Hymn to Wisdom and Closing Statement

century consumers of mainstream news, ready to declare guilt based on a 30-second video clip (or less), as though there can be no doubt or more information to gather.

Job says, "No thanks!" and, remarkably, appeals to the scariest judge possible: the Almighty. Job would rather appeal to him, knowing he is perfectly just. We also have good reason to think Job knows God as merciful and gracious (9:15).

In appealing to God rather than man, Job demonstrates the same wisdom as David. In David's case, the coming calamity WAS due to his sin (that of an unauthorized census issued by pride):

> **2 Samuel 24:11–14**
> **11** When David got up in the morning, the word of the LORD had come to the prophet Gad, David's seer: **12** "Go and say to David, 'This is what the LORD says: I am offering you three choices. Choose one of them, and I will do it to you.'"
> **13** So Gad went to David, told him the choices, and asked him, "Do you want three years of famine to come on your land, to flee from your foes three months while they pursue you, or to have a plague in your land three days? Now, consider carefully what answer I should take back to the one who sent me."
> **14** David answered Gad, "I have great anxiety. Please, let us fall into the LORD's hands because his mercies are great, but don't let me fall into human hands."

If David, whose punishment was directly due to sin, trusted in God's mercy, how much more was Job justified in doing so in his innocence? Job has adamantly laid it all on the line, invited curses upon himself if he has done any of the listed things deserving prosecution. Now, at the end of all this back-and-forth, Job says, "I rest my case."

Reflection
Why do you suppose Job uses such over-the-top language in his "if-then" statements of ch.31?

How many times does Job mention God in these statements, and why is that significant?

Since Job is using parallelism in v.35b and c, who is he calling his Opponent? Why is this ironic, given that satan means "opponent"?

Job: The Cry of the Righteous Sufferer

How can Job both say, "I would give him an account of all my steps" (v.37) and also have confidence in God's mercy? How can we?

How would you summarize Job's final position toward his friends? Toward God?

What has the story up to this point brought you to expect or hope for next?

Lesson 14 Dialogue: Elihu's Speeches 1 & 2 (Chs.32 - 34)

Job and his three friends have exhausted their arguments. It seems there is no clear winner to declare. The friends believe their case to be iron-clad, but Job is unyielding in his fight and has declared his resolution to the bitter end. But the bout is over, right? Not so! A fourth debater speaks up, and this is the first we have even heard of his presence!

Eli-who? the Angry Youngster

Job 32
1 So these three men quit answering Job, because he was righteous in his own eyes. **2** Then Elihu son of Barachel the Buzite from the family of Ram became angry. He was angry at Job because he had justified himself rather than God. **3** He was also angry at Job's three friends because they had failed to refute him and yet had condemned him. **4** Now Elihu had waited to speak to Job because they were all older than he. **5** But when he saw that the three men could not answer Job, he became angry.

Elihu's name seems appropriate. What are we to make of this sudden appearance, and who is this guy? It seems that Elihu has been there all along, for he will cite portions of the previous arguments and respond with his own commentary.

At least three mysteries arise. First, why did the writer not mention Elihu before? Second, why does God not mention him later? Third, why has Elihu not spoken up until now? The last question, Elihu will himself answer shortly. The second question we'll deal with later, when we consider what God says about all this. What of the first question? Why has the narrator not mentioned Elihu until now?

The initial statement about the visitation of Job's friends numbered three (2:11), and that language is repeated here. This makes one wonder why Elihu is not grouped in the category "friends." Perhaps it is because he is much younger, and not a peer. Some suggest he may have stood in the role of an adjudicator or an impartial mediator, and that's why he waited to speak and was not numbered with the friends. Perhaps Elihu was a local, even one of Job's proteges. It is even suggested Elihu may have been the writer of this book, and so kept himself anonymous until now. In any case, it seems the writer may have "sprung" Elihu upon us for literary purposes, to enhance the role of his statements to form a kind of bridge to the speeches of God that follow.

We are actually given more background about Elihu's lineage than about any of the three friends (v.2). His name means "He is my God." Gn 22:21 records a Buz who was one of Abraham's nephews (whose descendants would be Buzites), and Jeremiah (25:23) writes of a Buzite people group that may well connect to that line. There was a Ram who was an ancestor of David (Ruth 4:19-22), though it's impossible to tell if any of these lines connect in the case of this Elihu.

Job: The Cry of the Righteous Sufferer

So much for the youngster's sudden entrance and his identity. Will he have anything new to contribute to the discussion? Commentators observe that some of his remarks foreshadow God's own statements, providing a transitionary function. Here's Constable's assessment:

". . . the Elihu speeches (chaps. 32–37), which seemingly interrupt the argument of the book, actually set the stage for the Yahweh speeches. Elihu appears as a type of mediator (an impartial witness) who speaks on behalf of God (36:2) by rebuking the three friends (cf. 32:3, 6–14; 34:2–15; cf. 35:4) and by suggesting that Job needed to repent of his pride which developed because of his suffering (cf. 33:17; 35:12–16). He recommended that Job should exalt God's works which are evident in nature (36:24–37:18) and fear Him who comes in golden splendor out of the north (37:22–24). These basic ideas of Elihu are either assumed or developed by the Lord in His speeches."[12]

To draw again from our boxing analogy, what role does Elihu serve? Does he come in as a surprise contender to sit Job down? Does he barge in as a would-be trainer, to tell the friends, "This is how it's done"? Or is he a "hype man," bursting boisterously onto the scene to set the stage for the all-time champion, Yahweh the Great? Elihu seems to function as some combination of these, but likely most of all as the last option, the "hype man."

Though Elihu's speeches may function in all these ways, it is clear that his personal perspective is neither supernatural nor flawless. He is a man, and like the other men he will speak some truth and some error. His high view of God is applaudable. He may offer some appropriate rebukes to Job, but they still seem to be based on faulty assumptions, assigning stronger meaning than Job's statements probably warranted. His remarks may foreshadow God's own, but he still does not offer answers to Job's questions about why he is suffering for no apparent reason.

One particularly notable aspect of Elihu's introduction is his anger. Four times in just three verses the writer informs us he is angry.

With whom is Elihu angry, and why?

How does Elihu's statement in v.2b show us that he adopts the same either/or position of the three friends (that either Job is in the right or God is)?

---

[12] Constable, T. (2003). *Tom Constable's Expository Notes on the Bible* (Job 31:1). Galaxie Software.

Elihu's Speeches 1 & 2

Elihu's either/or view causes his frustration with both sides. He interprets Job's protests of innocence as accusations against God to a degree which Job never voiced. He interprets the failure of the friends to prove Job's guilt as an allowance that God might be wrong by default. He must do what the friends failed to do, to prove Job in the wrong. We will see that his attempts are more focused in the opposite direction, to do so indirectly. He will attempt to strongly and eloquently assert that God cannot be in the wrong, and therefore Job must be.

Elihu's First Speech

Toward All (Or to Anyone Who Will Listen):

"I must speak"
So, Elihu comes out of nowhere (from the reader's perspective) in a sort of rhetorical photobomb. He takes advantage of the silence to jump in unannounced and erupt onto everyone. Though he has remained silent (and to us completely invisible), he testifies that he can hold back no longer:

> **6** So Elihu son of Barachel the Buzite replied:
>
>> I am young in years,
>> while you are old;
>> therefore I was timid and afraid
>> to tell you what I know.
>> **7** I thought that age should speak
>> and maturity should teach wisdom.
>> **8** But it is the spirit in a person—
>> the breath from the Almighty—
>> that gives anyone understanding.
>> **9** It is not only the old who are wise
>> or the elderly who understand how to judge.
>> **10** Therefore I say, "Listen to me.
>> I too will declare what I know."
>> **11** Look, I waited for your conclusions;
>> I listened to your insights
>> as you sought for words.

Job: The Cry of the Righteous Sufferer

12 I paid close attention to you.
Yet no one proved Job wrong;
not one of you refuted his arguments.
13 So do not claim, "We have found wisdom;
let God deal with him, not man."
14 But Job has not directed his argument to me,
and I will not respond to him with your arguments.
15 Job's friends are dismayed and can no longer answer;
words have left them.
16 Should I continue to wait now that they are silent,
now that they stand there and no longer answer?
17 I too will answer;
yes, I will tell what I know.
18 For I am full of words,
and my spirit compels me to speak.
19 My heart is like unvented wine;
it is about to burst like new wineskins.
20 I must speak so that I can find relief;
I must open my lips and respond.
21 I will be partial to no one,
and I will not give anyone an undeserved title.
22 For I do not know how to give such titles;
otherwise, my Maker would remove me in an instant.

What reason does Elihu give for waiting to speak?

Why does he say he now will speak?

From what or whom does he say wisdom comes?

What evaluation does he offer in vv.11-15 about the collective argument of the three friends?

Elihu's Speeches 1 & 2

Elihu states a noble commitment in v.21. If he were to truly be an impartial third party, he might well satisfy Job's cry for exactly this kind of a mediator. If his inspiration (v.8) were flawless as delivered by an angelic messenger, he might really give Job some answers. Unfortunately, as we already observed and as his speeches will bear out, Elihu is a mere human. This means his best attempts to be impartial are doomed to fall short for one important reason. He does not have all the information to represent both parties (human and divine).

Just like the other men, Elihu does not know everything Job does about Job's own heart and motives. This means he cannot perfectly represent man as man. He may not willfully assert a bias against other men, but it resides within him nonetheless because he is not able to inspect or know their inward hearts. He can only be impartial regarding the external facts, and that is not enough here.

Elihu also does not know everything God does. This means he cannot represent God as God. He is not only ignorant of what God knows about men's hearts (including Job and all three friends). He is also ignorant of other factors, like what is discussed in heavenly councils, the purposes and activities of demonic opposition and the ultimate purposes of the sovereign Almighty. Elihu will talk a lot about God, but he doesn't know the facts that were given to us readers in chs.1-2. Once again, Elihu can only be impartial regarding the *external* facts, the visible ways God has revealed himself in his actions.

Toward Job:

"Refute me if you can"
So, Elihu carries out his strategy. He will begin by asserting that Job is in the wrong. Since he cannot address Job's inward person, this will have to be a bald claim based only on the external evidence to the "fact" that it must be so:

Job 33
> 1 But now, Job, pay attention to my speech,
> and listen to all my words.
> 2 I am going to open my mouth;
> my tongue will form words on my palate.
> 3 My words come from my upright heart,
> and my lips speak with sincerity what they know.
> 4 The Spirit of God has made me,
> and the breath of the Almighty gives me life.
> 5 Refute me if you can.
> Prepare your case against me; take your stand.
> 6 I am just like you before God;
> I was also pinched off from a piece of clay.

> **7** Fear of me should not terrify you;
> no pressure from me should weigh you down.
> **8** Surely you have spoken in my hearing,
> and I have heard these very words:
> **9** "I am pure, without transgression;
> I am clean and have no iniquity.
> **10** But he finds reasons to oppose me;
> he regards me as his enemy.
> **11** He puts my feet in the stocks;
> he stands watch over all my paths."

The line "Refute me if you can" is ironic, for Job could dare Elihu with the same words and with more success. Elihu can make such a strong invitation only because of his strategy to focus on God's perfection rather than offering direct evidence that Job is evil. He will not assert anything disagreeable about God, and so Job can't refute him in that, nor would Job wish to (since he would agree with every good statement about God).

"You are wrong in this matter"

Here Elihu makes his strategic pivot. He declares Job in the wrong, but does so by shifting the focus upon God's greatness:

> **12** But I tell you that you are wrong in this matter,
> since God is greater than man.
> **13** Why do you take him to court
> for not answering anything a person asks?

"God disciplines and restores"

The hype man declares God the greatest. Case closed. Why does Job keep demanding answers? Elihu now describes God's gracious pattern of discipline over his people. He speaks warning to them, he disciplines them, saves them and restores them:

> **14** For God speaks time and again,
> but a person may not notice it.
> **15** In a dream, a vision in the night,
> when deep sleep comes over people
> as they slumber on their beds,
> **16** he uncovers their ears
> and terrifies them with warnings,
> **17** in order to turn a person from his actions
> and suppress the pride of a person.

Elihu's Speeches 1&2

18 God spares his soul from the Pit,
his life from crossing the river of death.
19 A person may be disciplined on his bed with pain
and constant distress in his bones,
20 so that he detests bread,
and his soul despises his favorite food.
21 His flesh wastes away to nothing,
and his unseen bones stick out.
22 He draws near to the Pit,
and his life to the executioners.
23 If there is an angel on his side,
one mediator out of a thousand,
to tell a person what is right for him
24 and to be gracious to him and say,
"Spare him from going down to the Pit;
I have found a ransom,"
25 then his flesh will be healthier than in his youth,
and he will return to the days of his youthful vigor.
26 He will pray to God, and God will delight in him.
That person will see his face with a shout of joy,
and God will restore his righteousness to him.
27 He will look at men and say,
"I have sinned and perverted what was right;
yet I did not get what I deserved.
28 He redeemed my soul from going down to the Pit,
and I will continue to see the light."
29 God certainly does all these things
two or three times to a person
30 in order to turn him back from the Pit,
so he may shine with the light of life.

The strength of Elihu's argument here is that Job would not contest it. Who would argue that God does not discipline his own for their own good? Certainly not Job! Elihu has spoken of the righteous praying for restoration (v.26), and Job is the only one in this story explicitly known to have made prayer a consistent practice. We recall that Job was diligent in seeking God's mercy and redemption on behalf of his children (1:5), so we can be sure he practiced the same for himself.

What does Elihu imply about Job when speaking of God's discipline?

Job: The Cry of the Righteous Sufferer

Elihu brings up mediation again (v.23). He may well see himself in this role of mediator, a sort of angel delivering inspired council to Job. If so, we have seen that he falls short of what Job desires and really needs in a mediator.

Elihu does offer something here more helpful than the friends have. They spoke of (Job's) suffering in *punitive* terms. God uses it to punish, so Job should repent. Elihu speaks of suffering in *instructive* terms ("speak," v.14; "warnings," v.16; "turn," vv.17,30). God uses it to teach, so Job should learn from it. This idea anticipates James:

> **James 1:2–4**
> **2** Consider it a great joy, my brothers and sisters, whenever you experience various trials, **3** because you know that the testing of your faith produces endurance. **4** And let endurance have its full effect, so that you may be mature and complete, lacking nothing.

How does the idea of learning through suffering anticipate a major theme of this whole book?

With good reason to be confident, given his focus on indisputable truths about God, Elihu condescends to Job again:

> **31** Pay attention, Job, and listen to me.
> Be quiet, and I will speak.
> **32** But if you have something to say, answer me;
> speak, for I would like to justify you.
> **33** If not, then listen to me;
> be quiet, and I will teach you wisdom.

Elihu's Second Speech

Toward All Again:

Not surprisingly, when Elihu dares Job to speak up there is no response. Why would Job answer? He agrees with what Elihu has said about God, even if he disagrees with Elihu's overstated assertions about Job himself. So, since no one else jumps in, Elihu stands even taller on his soapbox to dispense wisdom to all:

Elihu's Speeches 1&2

"Let us judge for ourselves…"

Job 34
1 Then Elihu continued, saying:
2 Hear my words, you wise ones,
and listen to me, you knowledgeable ones.
3 Doesn't the ear test words
as the palate tastes food?
4 Let us judge for ourselves what is right;
let us decide together what is good.

How is Elihu right that we humans can to some extent – and are commanded to (1 Jn 4:1) – discern between right and wrong?

What is the problem, though, with men – even in community together – judging what is right and good? What key ingredient is missing in this formula?

Elihu's claim that men can judge for themselves what is right sounds more promising in the safety of community versus the discernment of one individual. In terms of human self-governance, it is the best we can do. By God's grace, all human societies, even the most pagan, have remarkably similar moral codes. Of course, every one of them fails to live up to the codes, and so those codes tend to degrade to match the culture.

The issue brought up here is at the fore of the whole matter of Job. A community of friends – and now a plus-one – is standing in judgment of one man, and they are getting it wrong. Why? Because, even with the best of intentions, when humans judge right and good for themselves, they are at best working in ignorance. At worst, they are inclined to twist the definitions to their good and to other's harm.

This is the Garden all over again. It is human fallenness. We the readers have known all along that these guys are missing the mark in their noble efforts to "test Job's words" and "judge what is right." We know this because of the information contained in a few short sentences. How remarkable is it that one tiny piece of information can completely change what we think is right!

Job: The Cry of the Righteous Sufferer

Elihu's Accurate Summary
Now that Elihu has invited the men to "decide together" in judgment, he restates Job's case in a brief summary:

> **5** For Job has declared, "I am righteous,
> yet God has deprived me of justice.
> **6** Would I lie about my case?
> My wound is incurable,
> though I am without transgression."

Once again, Elihu says nothing controversial. He has given a clear, concise and accurate representation of Job's argument (compare vv.5-6 with 10:7; 27:2 and 33:9). So far, so good. This summary is true.

Elihu's Distorted Assessment
But in the assessment, Elihu quickly repeats the errors of the friends. He distorts Job's statement, and then, based on that distortion, immediately mischaracterizes Job's whole manner of conduct:

> **7** What man is like Job?
> He drinks derision like water.
> **8** He keeps company with evildoers
> and walks with wicked men.
> **9** For he has said, "A man gains nothing
> when he becomes God's friend."

The statement Elihu attributes to Job in v.9 apparently refers to 21:15, where Job said, "Who is the Almighty, that we should serve him, and what will we gain by pleading with him?" Job put these words on the lips of the wicked in his rebuttal to Zophar. Job himself was not affirming this view, but pointing out that the wicked do, for they do not want to know God's ways (v.14). Job explicitly took the position opposite from the wicked when he said in v.16, "The counsel of the wicked is far from me!"

So, Elihu takes Job's statement out of context. Then he immediately draws conclusions based on that misunderstanding. Job is totally given over to the company of the wicked, following in their way of rebellion.

How have you seen people's statements (including your own) taken out of context to their harm?

Elihu's Speeches 1 & 2

"Could one who hates justice govern the world?"

His faulty premise notwithstanding, Elihu forges ahead assuming Job is a reprobate. He goes back to his strength, listing off statements that are absolutely true about God. It doesn't matter that Job himself agrees with these statements. They still are meant to serve as implications that Job must be in the wrong:

> **10** Therefore listen to me, you men of understanding.
> It is impossible for God to do wrong,
> and for the Almighty to act unjustly.
> **11** For he repays a person according to his deeds,
> and he gives him what his conduct deserves.
> **12** Indeed, it is true that God does not act wickedly
> and the Almighty does not pervert justice.
> **13** Who gave him authority over the earth?
> Who put him in charge of the entire world?
> **14** If he put his mind to it
> and withdrew the spirit and breath he gave,
> **15** every living thing would perish together
> and mankind would return to the dust.
> **16** If you have understanding, hear this;
> listen to what I have to say.
> **17** Could one who hates justice govern the world?
> Will you condemn the mighty Righteous One,
> **18** who says to a king, "Worthless man!"
> and to nobles, "Wicked men!"?
> **19** God is not partial to princes
> and does not favor the rich over the poor,
> for they are all the work of his hands.
> **20** They die suddenly in the middle of the night;
> people shudder, then pass away.
> Even the mighty are removed without effort.
> **21** For his eyes watch over a man's ways,
> and he observes all his steps.
> **22** There is no darkness, no deep darkness,
> where evildoers can hide.

The "you" in v.17b is singular, so the question, "Will you condemn the mighty Righteous One?" is aimed at Job. The question would also implicate the three friends, because in Elihu's opinion they have not silenced Job's argument and have therefore also implied that God is to blame.

But Elihu does no better. Commentators observe that his argument heads a dangerous direction in vv.10-15. If God sovereignly does everything that happens, and everything he does is right, then

Job: The Cry of the Righteous Sufferer

there is no such thing as evil. If God's ultimate power means he can do whatever he wants to his creatures, to the point of destroying them without cause, isn't that "might makes right"? This position seems to severely underestimate God's goodness and sterilize the true nature of his justice. It seems Elihu only brings us back to the problem of Retribution Theology.

Did Job ever in his speeches say, "God hates justice"? Has Job "condemned the Righteous One"?

What is it that forces Elihu to conclude that Job has implied these things?

"God does not need to examine a person...in court."

Job has more than once voiced his desire to argue his case before God (13:3; 23:3-7), though he has despaired of that hope. Not only does this seem unlikely, Elihu argues it is not necessary:

> **23** God does not need to examine a person further,
> that one should approach him in court.
> **24** He shatters the mighty without an investigation
> and sets others in their place.
> **25** Therefore, he recognizes their deeds
> and overthrows them by night, and they are crushed.
> **26** In full view of the public,
> he strikes them for their wickedness,
> **27** because they turned aside from following him
> and did not understand any of his ways
> **28** but caused the poor to cry out to him,
> and he heard the outcry of the needy.

What reason does Elihu give that God "shatters" and "overthrows" the mighty?

What does he say the poor and needy do?

Elihu's Speeches 1&2

In which category does Elihu seem to place Job?

"When God is silent"

If Elihu has taken a promising tack in arguing for God's greatness, he uses an even more shrewd strategy now. We might call it the "argument from silence":

> **29** But when God is silent, who can declare him guilty?
> When he hides his face, who can see him?
> Yet he watches over both individuals and nations,
> **30** so that godless men should not rule
> or ensnare the people.

Elihu makes a good point here, that God in his transcendence cannot be proven guilty of any misconduct. This emphasizes the point that God cannot be to blame for evil, whether generally or specifically in Job's case. It's too bad that Elihu cannot extrapolate that since God is beyond human purview it may be that others – say, satanic forces – are as well.

Toward Job Again:

"Suppose someone says"

Now, Elihu conducts a thought experiment, as though it should lead Job to repentance. Elihu takes Job to have disregarded God's attempts to get his attention. Job is not only unrepentant, but he actually blows God off:

> **31** Suppose someone says to God,
> "I have endured my punishment;
> I will no longer act wickedly.
> **32** Teach me what I cannot see;
> if I have done wrong, I won't do it again."
> **33** Should God repay you on your terms
> when you have rejected his?
> You must choose, not I!
> So declare what you know.
> **34** Reasonable men will say to me,
> along with the wise men who hear me,
> **35** "Job speaks without knowledge;
> his words are without insight."

Job: The Cry of the Righteous Sufferer

> **36** If only Job were tested to the limit,
> because his answers are like those of wicked men.
> **37** For he adds rebellion to his sin;
> he scornfully claps in our presence,
> while multiplying his words against God.

Funny thing, Job has already demonstrated the humble, submissive attitude Elihu suggests in vv.31-32. Job had said to Eliphaz, "Teach me and I will be silent. Help me understand what I did wrong" (6:24). Perhaps one could argue that Job was being sarcastic to his friend and not sincere. Fair enough. But it would be very difficult to make that argument when Job says virtually the same thing to God in ch.13:

> **22** Then call, and I will answer,
> or I will speak, and you can respond to me.
> **23** How many iniquities and sins have I committed?
> Reveal to me my transgression and sin.

Job has been truly humble before God. He has expressed a submissive heart, willing to repent of sin when appropriate. Why can Elihu and the friends not see that? They are still blinded by their theology of retribution. Job's trouble must be correction or punishment from God, and that means the only thing to make things right again is repentance. Job's vocalized *willingness* to repent is not enough. He must *actually* repent, and they have not heard him do so.

Reflection
Have you ever been frustrated when someone has misread your heart in a matter? How did you respond?

How difficult is it to hear truth from someone else when they are offering counsel from a faulty judgment? How important is it to realize that God still may be speaking to us through them?

Lesson 15 Dialogue: Elihu's Speeches 3 & 4 (Chs.35 - 37)

Elihu's Third Speech

We've already seen that Elihu's approach leaves much to be desired. He speaks too confidently about things he cannot know, namely, what is going on in Job's heart. Still, as it always is with human counselors, his imperfect delivery does not mean that there is not truth in what he says. God may be speaking to Job through this limited and imperfect counselor, so he (and we) must hear him out and find the meat but spit out the bones.

"If you are righteous, what do you give him?"
In the next chapter, Elihu responds to two of Job's questions. In doing so, he will misinterpret Job's words again. The first question is, "What does it profit me if I do not sin?"

> **Job 35**
> **1** Then Elihu continued, saying:
>
> **2** Do you think it is just when you say,
> "I am righteous before God"?
> **3** For you ask, "What does it profit you,
> and what benefit comes to me, if I do not sin?"
> **4** I will answer you
> and your friends with you.
> **5** Look at the heavens and see;
> gaze at the clouds high above you.
> **6** If you sin, how does it affect God?
> If you multiply your transgressions, what does it do to him?
> **7** If you are righteous, what do you give him,
> or what does he receive from your hand?
> **8** Your wickedness affects a person like yourself,
> and your righteousness, a son of man.

The line from v.3 essentially repeats the allegation from 34:9 ("a man gains nothing when he becomes God's friend"). The wording here seems to be a response to Job's words in 9:29, where he argued, "Since I will be found guilty, why should I struggle in vain?" The context there shows that Job was talking about the general truth that God's purity is absolute and far beyond man. He was not saying he was guilty in this particular case. As before, we see that Job has not declared he actually thinks being righteous is a waste. This is a distortion by Elihu.

What's more, Elihu doesn't provide a satisfactory answer. He ends up arguing that God is unaffected by man's moral choices (vv.7-8). This protects God's transcendence, but at the expense of his imminence. Instead of being impartial, now God is indifferent. This doesn't square with the notion that God interacts with men to teach them through discipline. This argument offers no solution, for if God is indifferent, he does not care about justice.

"God does not listen to empty cries"
The next question Elihu addresses is this: "Why does God not answer (Job's) prayers?":

> **9** People cry out because of severe oppression;
> they shout for help because of the power of the mighty.
> **10** But no one asks, "Where is God my Maker,
> who provides us with songs in the night,
> **11** who gives us more understanding than the animals of the earth
> and makes us wiser than the birds of the sky?"
> **12** There they cry out, but he does not answer,
> because of the pride of evil people.
> **13** Indeed, God does not listen to empty cries,
> and the Almighty does not take note of it—
> **14** how much less when you complain
> that you do not see him,
> that your case is before him
> and you are waiting for him.
> **15** But now, because God's anger does not punish
> and he does not pay attention to transgression,
> **16** Job opens his mouth in vain
> and multiplies words without knowledge.

Elihu's answer is cold and sterile. He essentially explains that Job is not getting answers because of his pride and complaining. God's silence is Job's fault. This conclusion is neither justified nor helpful.

What kinds of reasons are often offered to people for why their prayers don't seem to be answered?

Elihu's Fourth Speech

Toward All, Mostly (A Long Soliloquy):

Elihu's Speeches 3 & 4

"I will ascribe justice to my Maker"

Elihu turns back to his strategy of proclaiming – at length – God's greatness, and especially his justice. He seems to soften his tone once again. He also seems to assert once again that his knowledge is perfect knowledge from God:

Job 36
1 Then Elihu continued, saying:

> 2 Be patient with me a little longer, and I will inform you,
> for there is still more to be said on God's behalf.
> 3 I will get my knowledge from a distant place
> and ascribe justice to my Maker.
> 4 Indeed, my words are not false;
> one who has complete knowledge is with you.

Elihu sounds remarkably arrogant here. This does not tell us whether his words of "complete knowledge" will turn out to be true or not. We read on:

"God instructs them by their torment"

> 5 Yes, God is mighty, but he despises no one;
> he understands all things.
> 6 He does not keep the wicked alive,
> but he gives justice to the oppressed.
> 7 He does not withdraw his gaze from the righteous,
> but he seats them forever with enthroned kings,
> and they are exalted.
> 8 If people are bound with chains
> and trapped by the cords of affliction,
> 9 God tells them what they have done
> and how arrogantly they have transgressed.
> 10 He opens their ears to correction
> and tells them to repent from iniquity.
> 11 If they listen and serve him,
> they will end their days in prosperity
> and their years in happiness.
> 12 But if they do not listen,
> they will cross the river of death
> and die without knowledge.
> 13 Those who have a godless heart harbor anger;
> even when God binds them, they do not cry for help.

Job: The Cry of the Righteous Sufferer

> **14** They die in their youth;
> their life ends among male cult prostitutes.
> **15** God rescues the afflicted by their affliction;
> he instructs them by their torment.

Efforts throughout the long chapters of dialogue to trace Job's suffering back to a coherent understanding of justice have come up empty. We must look elsewhere for the explanation of the suffering of the innocent. Here Elihu begins to offer more of the possibility introduced earlier. God teaches through suffering. The godly learn from their suffering and are refined. The ungodly blame God and resent him.

"You have been tested by affliction"

Elihu turns his assertion toward Job as his own explanation for his suffering with a warning:

> **16** Indeed, he lured you from the jaws of distress
> to a spacious and unconfined place.
> Your table was spread with choice food.
> **17** Yet now you are obsessed with the judgment due the wicked;
> judgment and justice have seized you.
> **18** Be careful that no one lures you with riches;
> do not let a large ransom lead you astray.
> **19** Can your wealth or all your physical exertion
> keep you from distress?
> **20** Do not long for the night
> when nations will disappear from their places.
> **21** Be careful that you do not turn to iniquity,
> for that is why you have been tested by affliction.

Testing does not automatically imply sin, but what evidence do we have that Elihu thinks Job's testing is a direct result of personal wrongdoing?

"God is exalted, and you should praise his work"

Elihu goes back to his indisputable statements about God, and he can't help but coach Job about how he should be responding to God's awesome work (as though he is not):

> **22** Look, God shows himself exalted by his power.
> Who is a teacher like him?

Elihu's Speeches 3&4

23 Who has appointed his way for him,
and who has declared, "You have done wrong"?
24 Remember that you should praise his work,
which people have sung about.
25 All mankind has seen it;
people have looked at it from a distance.
26 Yes, God is exalted beyond our knowledge;
the number of his years cannot be counted.
27 For he makes waterdrops evaporate;
they distill the rain into its mist,
28 which the clouds pour out
and shower abundantly on mankind.
29 Can anyone understand how the clouds spread out
or how the thunder roars from God's pavilion?
30 See how he spreads his lightning around him
and covers the depths of the sea.
31 For he judges the nations with these;
he gives food in abundance.
32 He covers his hands with lightning
and commands it to hit its mark.
33 The thunder declares his presence;
the cattle also, the approaching storm.

Job 37

1 My heart pounds at this
and leaps from my chest.
2 Just listen to his thunderous voice
and the rumbling that comes from his mouth.
3 He lets it loose beneath the entire sky;
his lightning to the ends of the earth.
4 Then there comes a roaring sound;
God thunders with his majestic voice.
He does not restrain the lightning
when his rumbling voice is heard.
5 God thunders wondrously with his voice;
he does great things that we cannot comprehend.
6 For he says to the snow, "Fall to the earth,"
and the torrential rains, his mighty torrential rains,
7 serve as his sign to all mankind,
so that all men may know his work.
8 The wild animals enter their lairs
and stay in their dens.

> **9** The windstorm comes from its chamber,
> and the cold from the driving north winds.
> **10** Ice is formed by the breath of God,
> and watery expanses are frozen.
> **11** He saturates clouds with moisture;
> he scatters his lightning through them.
> **12** They swirl about,
> turning round and round at his direction,
> accomplishing everything he commands them
> over the surface of the inhabited world.
> **13** He causes this to happen for punishment,
> for his land, or for his faithful love.

While Elihu is getting it wrong about Job, he certainly is commendable for his high praise of God! There is a shift in the above verses from appreciation and exultation to expectation. Like the tension builds with an approaching storm, Elihu prepares us for an approaching theophany, an appearance of the Almighty. Such an appearance is often associated with a storm (Ex 19; Ps 18; Hab 3: Rv 4). Especially notable here is the description of thunder as the voice of God (cf. Jn 12:29; Rv 10:3-4). Elihu has "a moment" in v.1, in response to the approaching storm (36:33). As ch.37 unfolds, the storm moves in, swallowing up the debaters and us readers alike.

To Job (Mostly):

"Stop and consider God's wonders"
Elihu's speeches are drawing to a close, and as they do, he invites Job to share his wonder at God (not that he doesn't already). Job truly will wonder at God in the following chapters, far beyond what he would expect at this point. If Elihu's speeches serve as a bridge to those of God that will follow, then with these last words this is especially the case:

> **14** Listen to this, Job.
> Stop and consider God's wonders.
> **15** Do you know how God directs his clouds
> or makes their lightning flash?
> **16** Do you understand how the clouds float,
> those wonderful works of him who has perfect knowledge?
> **17** You whose clothes get hot
> when the south wind brings calm to the land,
> **18** can you help God spread out the skies
> as hard as a cast metal mirror?
> **19** Teach us what we should say to him;
> we cannot prepare our case because of our darkness.

Elihu's Speeches 3&4

> **20** Should he be told that I want to speak?
> Can a man speak when he is confused?
> **21** Now no one can even look at the sun
> when it is in the skies,
> after a wind has swept through and cleared the sky.
> **22** Out of the north he comes, shrouded in a golden glow;
> awesome majesty surrounds him.
> **23** The Almighty—we cannot reach him—
> he is exalted in power!
> He will not violate justice and abundant righteousness,
> **24** therefore, men fear him.
> He does not look favorably on any who are wise in heart.

It seems the storm has broken into peaceful blue skies with puffy clouds and sunshine too bright for the eyes. No, it is not the sun that is too bright to behold – it is God's glory! The stage is set. There are still unanswered questions, but they may be starting to fade into the periphery against this blinding eyeful of God's presence.

What have you found praiseworthy or useful in Elihu's speech? What has been frustrating? Does it seem to have advanced the dialogue in any way? If so, how?

What has struck you most about the impending glory of God as described here? As described in the NT, especially looking forward to the return of Christ?

Lesson 16 Dialogue: Job's Humiliation by God, Round One (Ch.38 – Ch.40, V.5)

Elihu was right that God does teach his people through suffering. The problem was with Elihu's assertion that God was causing Job's suffering as correction for sin. There was a real lack of tenderness in the speeches of Elihu and the three friends. The men all seemed to share one goal, to shock Job with irrefutable arguments and get him back in line. This goal, of course, presupposed that Job was *out* of line with God, a presupposition we as readers know was wrong, at least in the ways and to the degree asserted by Job's opponents. Still, convinced as they were, they felt justified in their attempts to shame Job into confession and repentance. This explains why every time Job protested that he was innocent, they redoubled their efforts to humiliate him.

Different Kinds of Humiliation
We know that before the friends ever showed up there were already attempts underway to shame Job. Satan, the Mad Scientist, had thrown everything he had at Job to humiliate him, and to prove his hypothesis that Job was undeserving of God's blessing. Job, the greatest man of all the people of the east, had been brought low by these attacks. First Satan humiliated him, and then his friends came to pile on even more shame.

Now the moment Job has waited for, cried out for – but barely dared to hope for – has arrived. The LORD himself shows up. We will see that God humiliates Job too. But this humiliation will be different. The speeches given by the LORD are given from complete understanding, with all wisdom and in perfect love and grace. Satan's goal was to destroy. The goal of the four men was better intended, as they sought to defend God's righteousness (though from a limited and legal perspective) and (they think) to pressure Job back into a state of godliness. But their attempts were not only misguided on Job's part but also harsh and even cruel.

When Yahweh humiliates Job it is overwhelming, and it is humbling, but it is not out of spite. God knows exactly what's going on here. He has allowed it for his purposes. And, yes, Elihu was right that God will teach and refine Job through this. But this has not been God's punishment, and he does not show up to punish Job now. He will remind Job of his humble status as a mere human. He will challenge Job, even to the point of a rebuke. But he will also vindicate him before his friends. Job's suffering may have pressed him to a point of a sinful *response*, but it did not come *because* he had sinned.

In a way, Job is like Jacob. He is wrestling with God, desperate for blessing – in Job's case *restored* blessing. He too is suffering injury, his own being far greater than a dislocated hip. Yet he too may persevere through his struggle and find in a very personal encounter with God the very thing he most desires.

Job: The Cry of the Righteous Sufferer

Bookends to the Dialogue

The long dialogue section of this book comes to a close with a pattern like that of the first chapters. There are two exchanges between Yahweh and Job, just as there were two between Yahweh and Satan. Just as those in the heavenly court give account to God in chs.1-2, so now Job must give account in chs.38-42. There are many other echoes from the earlier chapters, and we will explore some of them as we go through these last four speeches.

The LORD's First Speech

From the Whirlwind

> **Job 38**
> **1** Then the LORD answered Job from the whirlwind.

It is worth pausing to note the implications of this statement. First, we see Job is getting what he asked for, an audience with God. It will not go as he expected, however. Job's appeal was legal, as though God would come as a defendant to explain himself. Coming in a whirlwind sets the tone of God as almighty in this exchange. He comes not in defense but instead as the prosecutor, though his response is not legal but personal.

Whirlwinds elsewhere in Scripture are associated with God's presence (Ps 77:18; Ez 1:4) or heaven's breaking in as with Elijah's taking up (2 Kg 2:11). It is associated with calamity (Jb 9:17) and especially judgment (Prv 1:27; 10:25; Is 40:24; 41:16; 66:15; Jr 23:19; Ez 13:11,13; Hos 8:7; Nah 1:3; Zec 7:14). Given the accusations of the three friends, they may well have thought this would be the end of Job!

The whirlwind also reminds us of the great wind that took Job's most precious blessings, his children (1:19). How this moment must have rattled Job! Still, that wind of ch.1 was a destructive one that passed through, sweeping away his loved ones. This wind is under control and is stationary, a manifestation of the Almighty and his power. Job must trust that God's presence is not aimed at destroying him.

How are life's other storms different from a "God" storm?

Answering with Questions

So, the LORD does humble Job, but not like the others did. The LORD does at long last answer Job, but not in the way he expected. He does not answer his questions (*why all this?*) but rattles off a huge string of his own questions. These are rhetorical ones designed to swallow up all mortal questions with one answer. God will present himself as the Answer for all life's tests.

Job's Humiliation by God: Round One

"Who is this...?"

He said:

> **2** Who is this who obscures my counsel
> with ignorant words?
> **3** Get ready to answer me like a man;
> when I question you, you will inform me.

The question echoes the accusations of Elihu about Job (34:35; 35:16) but with a different texture. Elihu implied that Job's ignorance was due to the spiritual darkness of rebellion. God does not go that far, stating simply that Job is in the dark because of his severely limited perspective. Job is in the dark generally, then, but not morally. Elihu's implication amounts to what Paul described in Rm 1:

> **21** For though they knew God, they did not glorify him as God or show gratitude. Instead, their thinking became worthless, and their senseless hearts were darkened. **22** Claiming to be wise, they became fools **23** and exchanged the glory of the immortal God for images resembling mortal man, birds, four-footed animals, and reptiles.

How is Job's ignorance different from that of the darkened hearts mentioned by Paul?

Still, God's statement is a strong rebuke, because obscuring God's perfect counsel or wisdom with speeches from an ignorant perspective is still very dangerous and irresponsible. This limited perspective is in view with the announcement of v.3, that Job will answer God like a man. This verse is repeated verbatim in 40:7, at the beginning of the LORD's second speech.

To "answer like a man" might be taken as an idiom, like we would say, *"Take it like a man."* It may also be taken literally to refer to Job's vastly inferior status as a created being. This would be reinforced by a potentially sarcastic, "You will inform me" (v.3) and a surely sarcastic, "Certainly you know!" (v.5). Either way, or collectively, the point is clear: Job has demanded answers from a position of weakness but now God will demand answers from a position of absolute strength. This reminds us that Job, as a man, is accountable to God just as the sons of God are in chs.1-2.

"Where were you...?"
No doubt, God is intent on humbling Job. So, now that the rhetorical pump has been primed with the question of v.2, it gushes out a flood of questions for which Job cannot utter a reply. These focus on God's sovereign power to create and establish, to sustain and rule his creation, and to provide for his creatures:

Job: The Cry of the Righteous Sufferer

> **4** Where were you when I established the earth?
> Tell me, if you have understanding.
> **5** Who fixed its dimensions? Certainly you know!
> Who stretched a measuring line across it?
> **6** What supports its foundations?
> Or who laid its cornerstone
> **7** while the morning stars sang together
> and all the sons of God shouted for joy?
>
> **8** Who enclosed the sea behind doors
> when it burst from the womb,
> **9** when I made the clouds its garment
> and total darkness its blanket,
> **10** when I determined its boundaries
> and put its bars and doors in place,
> **11** when I declared, "You may come this far, but no farther;
> your proud waves stop here"?
>
> **12** Have you ever in your life commanded the morning
> or assigned the dawn its place,
> **13** so it may seize the edges of the earth
> and shake the wicked out of it?
> **14** The earth is changed as clay is by a seal;
> its hills stand out like the folds of a garment.
> **15** Light is withheld from the wicked,
> and the arm raised in violence is broken.

What verbs in these verses describe God's activities in creating and ruling?

"Do you know...?"
God goes on to speak of matters inaccessible to man's wisdom or control:

> **16** Have you traveled to the sources of the sea
> or walked in the depths of the oceans?
> **17** Have the gates of death been revealed to you?
> Have you seen the gates of deep darkness?
> **18** Have you comprehended the extent of the earth?
> Tell me, if you know all this.

Job's Humiliation by God: Round One

19 Where is the road to the home of light?
Do you know where darkness lives,
20 so you can lead it back to its border?
Are you familiar with the paths to its home?
21 Don't you know? You were already born;
you have lived so long!
22 Have you entered the place where the snow is stored?
Or have you seen the storehouses of hail,
23 which I hold in reserve for times of trouble,
for the day of warfare and battle?
24 What road leads to the place where light is dispersed?
Where is the source of the east wind that spreads across the earth?

25 Who cuts a channel for the flooding rain
or clears the way for lightning,
26 to bring rain on an uninhabited land,
on a desert with no human life,
27 to satisfy the parched wasteland
and cause the grass to sprout?
28 Does the rain have a father?
Who fathered the drops of dew?
29 Whose womb did the ice come from?
Who gave birth to the frost of heaven
30 when water becomes as hard as stone,
and the surface of the watery depths is frozen?

31 Can you fasten the chains of the Pleiades
or loosen the belt of Orion?
32 Can you bring out the constellations in their season
and lead the Bear and her cubs?
33 Do you know the laws of heaven?
Can you impose its authority on earth?
34 Can you command the clouds
so that a flood of water covers you?
35 Can you send out lightning bolts, and they go?
Do they report to you, "Here we are"?

36 Who put wisdom in the heart
or gave the mind understanding?
37 Who has the wisdom to number the clouds?
Or who can tilt the water jars of heaven

Job: The Cry of the Righteous Sufferer

> **38** when the dust hardens like cast metal
> and the clods of dirt stick together?

What things listed above are beyond man's understanding and reach?

God now moves to earthly phenomena that are much nearer to man's experience but that are still beyond his knowledge and control:

> **39** Can you hunt prey for a lioness
> or satisfy the appetite of young lions
> **40** when they crouch in their dens
> and lie in wait within their lairs?
> **41** Who provides the raven's food
> when its young cry out to God
> and wander about for lack of food?

Job 39

> **1** Do you know when mountain goats give birth?
> Have you watched the deer in labor?
> **2** Can you count the months they are pregnant
> so you can know the time they give birth?
> **3** They crouch down to give birth to their young;
> they deliver their newborn.
> **4** Their offspring are healthy and grow up in the open field.
> They leave and do not return.
>
> **5** Who set the wild donkey free?
> Who released the swift donkey from its harness?
> **6** I made the desert its home,
> and the salty wasteland its dwelling.
> **7** It scoffs at the noise of the village
> and never hears the shouts of a driver.
> **8** It roams the mountains for its pastureland,
> searching for anything green.
> **9** Would the wild ox be willing to serve you?
> Would it spend the night by your feeding trough?
> **10** Can you hold the wild ox to a furrow by its harness?
> Will it plow the valleys behind you?

Job's Humiliation by God: Round One

11 Can you depend on it because its strength is great?
Would you leave it to do your hard work?
12 Can you trust the wild ox to harvest your grain
and bring it to your threshing floor?

13 The wings of the ostrich flap joyfully,
but are her feathers and plumage like the stork's?
14 She abandons her eggs on the ground
and lets them be warmed in the sand.
15 She forgets that a foot may crush them
or that some wild animal may trample them.
16 She treats her young harshly, as if they were not her own,
with no fear that her labor may have been in vain.
17 For God has deprived her of wisdom;
he has not endowed her with understanding.
18 When she proudly spreads her wings,
she laughs at the horse and its rider.

19 Do you give strength to the horse?
Do you adorn his neck with a mane?
20 Do you make him leap like a locust?
His proud snorting fills one with terror.
21 He paws in the valley and rejoices in his strength;
he charges into battle.
22 He laughs at fear, since he is afraid of nothing;
he does not run from the sword.
23 A quiver rattles at his side,
along with a flashing spear and a javelin.
24 He charges ahead with trembling rage;
he cannot stand still at the sound of the ram's horn.
25 When the ram's horn blasts, he snorts defiantly.
He smells the battle from a distance;
he hears the officers' shouts and the battle cry.

26 Does the hawk take flight by your understanding
and spread its wings to the south?
27 Does the eagle soar at your command
and make its nest on high?
28 It lives on a cliff where it spends the night;
its stronghold is on a rocky crag.

Job: The Cry of the Righteous Sufferer

> **29** From there it searches for prey;
> its eyes penetrate the distance.
> **30** Its brood gulps down blood,
> and where the slain are, it is there.

How do these verses speak of God's provision and oversight? His benevolence?

In what ways do all these descriptions of God's activity humble a mere mortal?

When you stop to think about it, how much of your own experience is beyond your wisdom or control? How do you react to that? How <u>should</u> you?

"Will you correct the Almighty?"

> **Job 40**
> **1** The Lord answered Job:
>
> **2** Will the one who contends with the Almighty correct him?
> Let him who argues with God give an answer.

God's first speech seems overwhelming. It has been cosmic in scale and cutting to the natural pride in man. God even uses some biting sarcasm: "Certainly you know!" (38:5); "Don't you know? You were already born; you have lived so long!" (v.21). God describes the ostrich he has created for his own amusement, and says he has "deprived her of wisdom" (39:17). Perhaps this is a dig at Job who is like an ignorant beast compared to God. *Do you do this? Can you do that? Do you know how this works?*

This conversation happens a thousand times a day between humans. The mother educating the child. The boss straightening out the employee. The prof bringing decades of study to bear on the green freshman student. The hall-of-fame coach managing superstar egos. We get it.

Job's Humiliation by God: Round One

But this is a totally different category. This is that times infinity. This is the Creator of everything wiping the know-it-all smirk off the face of the puny creature who would cease to exist the instant that Creator ceased to will his creature's being. It is only by God's grace that Job lives and moves and has his being (Ac 17:28). It is in God's grace that he now speaks to Job, but that does not mean that his speech is soft or without rebuke. With that in mind, consider these questions:

Does this speech by God strike you as harsh? Why, or why not?

What does the tone of this first speech imply about Job? Does it feel like a rebuke?

Job's First Response: Humble Silence

If we are surprised at the tone of God's first speech, we may be even more surprised by Job's response:

> **3** Then Job answered the LORD:
>
> **4** I am so insignificant. How can I answer you?
> I place my hand over my mouth.
> **5** I have spoken once, and I will not reply;
> twice, but now I can add nothing.

What seems appropriate about Job's response?

Does it seem that anything is missing from this response? Why, or why not?

At first glance, Job's response is totally appropriate. He admits his relative insignificance. *Message received. I am humbled.* Speechlessness seems appropriate too. What could Job possibly say?

Commentators see something more here, and the gesture of v.4b – placing a hand over his mouth – is a clue. The interpretive pattern for the gesture in this book comes from 29:9, where Job was describing his glory days:

Job 29:7–11
> **7** When I went out to the city gate
> and took my seat in the town square,
> **8** the young men saw me and withdrew,
> while older men stood to their feet.
> **9** City officials stopped talking
> and covered their mouths with their hands.
> **10** The noblemen's voices were hushed,
> and their tongues stuck to the roof of their mouths.
> **11** When they heard me, they blessed me,
> and when they saw me, they spoke well of me.

This gesture is one of deference to a higher authority or wisdom, but not necessarily complete agreement with it or a wholehearted submission to it. The meaning of the gesture is heightened by its other use in Job:

Job 21:4–6
> **4** As for me, is my complaint against a human being?
> Then why shouldn't I be impatient?
> **5** Look at me and shudder;
> put your hand over your mouth.
> **6** When I think about it, I am terrified
> and my body trembles in horror.

Job indicates that Zophar would be appalled to think that Job would issue a complaint against God. The friend would cover his mouth as a representative move on Job's behalf to say, "Job, you have overstepped your bounds!"

There seems to be a quiet stubbornness in the case of this use in ch.40. While Job is recognizing the proper boundaries of humility by covering his mouth, he is not as yet backing off his claims that God has treated him unjustly. Job's words still hang in the air: "I call for help, but there is no justice" (19:7); "As God lives, who has deprived me of justice…" (27:2).

All this is to say that Job's first response indicates that his suffering has not quite yet yielded its full work of maturing him. So far, he is expressing humility that is appropriate, but he has not yet surrendered his legal claim of injustice. His position now echoes what he said earlier:

Job's Humiliation by God: Round One

Job 9:14–17
> **14** How then can I answer him
> or choose my arguments against him?
> **15** Even if I were in the right, I could not answer.
> I could only beg my Judge for mercy.
> **16** If I summoned him and he answered me,
> I do not believe he would pay attention to what I said.
> **17** He batters me with a whirlwind
> and multiplies my wounds without cause.

Job is refraining from further speech because of God's overwhelming power. That is not quite the same as saying yet that he is satisfied. His silence may not be any more than a natural response to avoid retribution, as he voiced earlier:

Job 31:23
> **23** For disaster from God terrifies me,
> and because of his majesty I could not do these things.

So, Job's humble silence is appropriate but there are signs of more work to do, more movement to come in Job's heart. God's first speech was an objective presentation of his majestic establishment and rule of the cosmos, but it did not really deal with his justice. He has not directly accused Job of sin, but he has given him quite a dressing down! Job's friends are probably amazed that God has not struck Job dead, but Job seems to still be quietly waiting for God to explain why he has caused him all this pain for no apparent reason. None of the men will get what they expect, but Job will finally be satisfied in a way he did not anticipate.

Lesson 17 Dialogue: Job's Humiliation by God, Round Two
(Ch.40, V6 – Ch.42, V.6)

The LORD's Second Speech

"Would you really challenge my justice?"
Yahweh's first speech was an overwhelming challenge, to be sure. God is the all-powerful Creator. His power to establish, direct, and sustain everything is beyond understanding. He demonstrated that he is all-wise. Now we get to the key question of the entire series of dialogues: *Is he just?* God has shown that Job is unable to control the *natural* realm. Now he will demonstrate that he is also unable to control the *moral* realm. All creatures must trust God to carry out justice:

> **Job 40:6-9**
> **6** Then the LORD answered Job from the whirlwind:
>
> > **7** Get ready to answer me like a man;
> > When I question you, you will inform me.
> > **8** Would you really challenge my justice?
> > Would you declare me guilty to justify yourself?
> > **9** Do you have an arm like God's?
> > Can you thunder with a voice like his?

The pattern repeats. The LORD speaks again from the whirlwind. He repeats his challenge: "When I question you, you will inform me." Job is still a mere man who will give account to his sovereign Creator.

This time, God doesn't ask, "Who is this who obscures my counsel with ignorant words?" This time he is more direct with Job. The second line of poetry in v.8 clarifies the meaning of the first. Job has not explicitly called God unjust. He wouldn't dare, and it seems he doesn't really believe it to be true. But in protesting his own innocence and in questioning God's refusal to speak or act on his behalf, he has implied injustice. This was not lost on the friends, and Elihu interpreted it the same way (32:2). God here affirms that Job has gone too far in his protests of innocence. He has made it sound like God is culpable in his suffering, and that cannot be so.

"Your own right hand can deliver you."
In his first speech, God had demonstrated his transcendent wisdom. Now, God will focus on his power to execute his justice over every proud person. He is more than able to do what man cannot, to judge the proud and bring salvation from suffering:

Job: The Cry of the Righteous Sufferer

> **10** Adorn yourself with majesty and splendor,
> and clothe yourself with honor and glory.
> **11** Pour out your raging anger;
> look on every proud person and humiliate him.
> **12** Look on every proud person and humble him;
> trample the wicked where they stand.
> **13** Hide them together in the dust;
> imprison them in the grave.
> **14** Then I will confess to you
> that your own right hand can deliver you.

Anderson makes a profound point about this section:

> *Men are eager to use force to combat evil and in their impatience they wish God would do the same more often. But by such destructive acts men do and become evil. To behave as God suggests in 40:8–14, Job would not only usurp the role of God, he would become another Satan. Only God can destroy creatively. Only God can transmute evil into good. As Creator, responsible for all that happens in his world, he is able to make everything (good and bad) work together into good.*[13]

Since only God can ensure justice in all cases, this means that man has but one choice and one hope. He must trust God without reservation. Whether answers come or not, God alone must be trusted to deliver justice or there is no hope for it at all.

How have you found you are frustrated and helpless to stop other people from doing wrong?

How does God's challenge to Job here remind you that these things are too big for you, that you need a Savior to deliver justice?

"Can anyone capture Behemoth?"

Since providing justice requires supreme power, God goes on to confront Job with the overwhelming obstacles that must be overcome. He uses two creatures to depict the height of power on land and in the sea. Only one so great as to subdue these proudest of all creatures could have the power to ensure justice in ruling the world. These depictions seem to describe literal

---

[13] Andersen, F. I. (1976). *Job: An Introduction and Commentary* (Vol. 14, p. 310). Downers Grove, IL: InterVarsity Press.

creatures that are exaggerated to mythical proportions to illustrate the height of beastly arrogant power. (See Ps 104 for a similar passage in which the LORD is blessed because he alone masters all creatures.)

The first proud beast sounds like a fusion of animals similar to a hippopotamus, or perhaps even some great dinosaur. The term, "Behemoth" is actually a plural term meaning "beasts," which supports the idea that this creature is presented as an amalgam of huge land creatures.

> **15** Look at Behemoth,
> which I made along with you.
> He eats grass like cattle.
> **16** Look at the strength of his back
> and the power in the muscles of his belly.
> **17** He stiffens his tail like a cedar tree;
> the tendons of his thighs are woven firmly together.
> **18** His bones are bronze tubes;
> his limbs are like iron rods.
> **19** He is the foremost of God's works;
> only his Maker can draw the sword against him.
> **20** The hills yield food for him,
> while all sorts of wild animals play there.
> **21** He lies under the lotus plants,
> hiding in the protection of marshy reeds.
> **22** Lotus plants cover him with their shade;
> the willows by the brook surround him.
> **23** Though the river rages, Behemoth is unafraid;
> he remains confident, even if the Jordan surges up to his mouth.
> **24** Can anyone capture him while he looks on,
> or pierce his nose with snares?

Verse 19 serves to summarize the point of this section: "Only his Maker can draw the sword against him." The translations vary whether the "sword" is God's or Behemoth's (tooth), but the point is that only the Maker can draw near to him or subdue him. Only God can control Behemoth. He can lead this danger (by the nose, v.24) wherever he desires.

"Can you pull in Leviathan with a hook?"

God then moves to an even more extended description of the most terrible sea creature. "Leviathan" means "twisted animal" and is a term found in both ancient myth and elsewhere in the Bible. Canaanites had a seven-headed version. The description is the longest of any animal in the book. If it is of a literal animal, it is probably some kind of crocodile that is amplified by hyperbole. Taken mythologically, it describes a fire-breathing sea dragon. Carried to the utmost, this creature may even be associated with the highest power that opposes God, Satan himself (Is 27:1 with Rv 12:9-15; 20:2).

Job 41

1 Can you pull in Leviathan with a hook
or tie his tongue down with a rope?
2 Can you put a cord through his nose
or pierce his jaw with a hook?
3 Will he beg you for mercy
or speak softly to you?
4 Will he make a covenant with you
so that you can take him as a slave forever?
5 Can you play with him like a bird
or put him on a leash for your girls?
6 Will traders bargain for him
or divide him among the merchants?
7 Can you fill his hide with harpoons
or his head with fishing spears?
8 Lay a hand on him.
You will remember the battle
and never repeat it!
9 Any hope of capturing him proves false.
Does a person not collapse at the very sight of him?
10 No one is ferocious enough to rouse Leviathan;
who then can stand against me?
11 Who confronted me, that I should repay him?
Everything under heaven belongs to me.

12 I cannot be silent about his limbs,
his power, and his graceful proportions.
13 Who can strip off his outer covering?
Who can penetrate his double layer of armor?
14 Who can open his jaws,
surrounded by those terrifying teeth?
15 His pride is in his rows of scales,
closely sealed together.
16 One scale is so close to another
that no air can pass between them.
17 They are joined to one another,
so closely connected they cannot be separated.

Job's Humiliation by God: Round Two

18 His snorting flashes with light,
while his eyes are like the rays of dawn.
19 Flaming torches shoot from his mouth;
fiery sparks fly out!
20 Smoke billows from his nostrils
as from a boiling pot or burning reeds.
21 His breath sets coals ablaze,
and flames pour out of his mouth.
22 Strength resides in his neck,
and dismay dances before him.
23 The folds of his flesh are joined together,
solid as metal and immovable.
24 His heart is as hard as a rock,
as hard as a lower millstone!
25 When Leviathan rises, the mighty are terrified;
they withdraw because of his thrashing.
26 The sword that reaches him will have no effect,
nor will a spear, dart, or arrow.
27 He regards iron as straw,
and bronze as rotten wood.
28 No arrow can make him flee;
slingstones become like stubble to him.
29 A club is regarded as stubble,
and he laughs at the sound of a javelin.
30 His undersides are jagged potsherds,
spreading the mud like a threshing sledge.
31 He makes the depths seethe like a cauldron;
he makes the sea like an ointment jar.
32 He leaves a shining wake behind him;
one would think the deep had gray hair!
33 He has no equal on earth—
a creature devoid of fear!
34 He surveys everything that is haughty;
he is king over all the proud beasts.

What are some of the descriptions that show the outrageous futility of opposing these beasts?

What do you think Job is supposed to realize through these descriptions?

Job: The Cry of the Righteous Sufferer

The symbolic function of these beasts seems amplified in the second. Behemoth is "confident" (40:23), but Leviathan is "haughty" and king over all the "proud" beasts (41:34).

The point is vivid enough with a hippo or a croc, but even more so with any of these exaggerations. Man does not have the power to catch, let alone tame, these powerful beasts, so he is infinitely more outmatched against God. More to the point of Job's struggle, man is helpless against the powerful and beastly forces of pride and wickedness in this world. But even in the case of Satan himself (who is a force in chs.1-2 whether or not he is in mind here in ch.41), God has absolute power to control and ensure justice. He alone can deliver those who are helpless otherwise.

What a climax! God speaks from a whirlwind to articulate his absolute power over all creation. He builds to a long description of the most insurmountable forces of nature to show that it is hopeless to trust in anyone but the Almighty. Job wants justice and comfort for his suffering. He can hope in no one else. Only God has the power to turn everything for good.

How will Job respond now? Will he be satisfied?

Job's Second Response: Confession and Repentance

> **Job 42:1–6**
> **1** Then Job replied to the LORD:
>
> > **2** I know that you can do anything
> > and no plan of yours can be thwarted.
> > **3** You asked, "Who is this who conceals my counsel with ignorance?"
> > Surely I spoke about things I did not understand,
> > things too wondrous for me to know.
> > **4** You said, "Listen now, and I will speak.
> > When I question you, you will inform me."
> > **5** I had heard reports about you,
> > but now my eyes have seen you.
> > **6** Therefore, I reject my words and am sorry for them;
> > I am dust and ashes.

What does Job confess in vv.1-5?

How does Job's response go farther this time than in ch.40?

Job's Humiliation by God: Round Two

Have you ever been overzealous with your words and had to walk them back? What was that like?

Mission accomplished. God's presence has broken through and satisfied the cry of Job's suffering heart. Job did not get answers to his questions, but he is satisfied with something far greater. He has seen the LORD. He now beholds God's utter greatness and gives all his questions and frustrations over to complete trust in the only one powerful enough to rule and to save.

In v.2 Job acknowledges God's absolute sovereign power in contrast to all would-be opposition. Notice he first is overwhelmed by the *positive* assertion. In v.3 Job acknowledges God's absolute wisdom in contrast to his own ignorance. Observe that these transcendent realities are too *wonderful* rather than too *terrible*. In vv.4-5 Job is moved to pure awe and wonder. Job is satisfied. His reaction now parrots that of ch.1. It is worship. He wanted answers that were above his pay grade. What he got was the presence of the LORD. The Creator of the universe came and spoke to him, just as he had longed for:

Job 19:25–27
> **25** But I know that my Redeemer lives,
> and at the end he will stand on the dust.
> **26** Even after my skin has been destroyed,
> yet I will see God in my flesh.
> **27** I will see him myself;
> my eyes will look at him, and not as a stranger.
> My heart longs within me.

Now it has happened, and that was enough. His faith has grown. His perspective has been stretched. As commentator Carl Schultz observes, Job's suffering is no longer oriented around the "why" but the "how."[14] God's ways are higher than man's ways. He is either worthy of trust or he is not. Of course, Job rightly concludes the former.

Job's stubbornness has dissolved. This time he rejects his words and repents (the word translated "sorry" in the CSB). It is important to realize what this repentance does and does not mean. It cannot mean Job is repenting for any sin that has brought on his suffering, or the entire story collapses. It cannot mean that Job is admitting he has violated his integrity, or his friends are proven correct. P. Zuck puts it this way: *"Job admitted sinning because he suffered, but he did not admit that he was suffering because he had sinned."*[15]

---

[14] Schultz, C. (1995). Job. In *Evangelical Commentary on the Bible* (Vol. 3, p. 363). Grand Rapids, MI: Baker Book House.
[15] Constable, T. (2003). *Tom Constable's Expository Notes on the Bible* (Job 42:1). Galaxie Software.

Job: The Cry of the Righteous Sufferer

Job's repentance must be understood relative to his rejection of his own words in v.6. It must mean he has overstated his case at God's expense. He has spoken with too much confidence about things that were beyond him (v.3). Job is admitting he has made the same mistake as his friends. He opened his mouth and out of ignorance said too much. Just as the friends served him best at first with their quiet presence, Job realizes now that his own quiet trust in the presence of God should have been enough for him. His lesson becomes ours. Thomas Constable puts it this way:

"Our suffering may be due to our sin, as Job's three friends said, or because God wants to teach us something, as Elihu affirmed. However suffering may not be our lot for these reasons. When we cannot determine why we are suffering we can still rest in God and continue to trust and obey Him because we know He is sovereign and loving."[16]

Job has received his gift from the LORD. He has not been thundered upon as the friends or Elihu would expect. Nor has he been brought into the know with us readers about the cosmic origins of his suffering. He has been humbled by his God, and this has been a kindness. God has honored him with a special revelation of his near presence, and Job has humbly submitted to his sovereign rule.

How have you been humbled by circumstances that were out of your control?

How has God revealed himself to you in your own whirlwinds?

Have you ever been stubborn when God didn't give you "why" answers for your struggles?

How have you found comfort in knowing God is in control and wants what is best for you?

---

[16] Constable, T. (2003). <u>Tom Constable's Expository Notes on the Bible</u> (Job 42:1). Galaxie Software.

Lesson 18 Epilogue: Job's Integrity, Intercession and Greater Blessing (Ch.42, Vv.7 - 17)

What a journey! Job has gone from being the "greatest man among all the people of the east" to being a pitiful wretch in dust and ashes who is scorned by even his wife and closest friends. And now, after a long series of passionate debates, Job has been given a rare gift. He has experienced a special revelation of Yahweh that is so overwhelming that all his questions and frustrations melt away into worship. Job has confessed God's surpassing greatness and has repented of being too zealous in defending his own reputation over God's. He has submitted to God's mysterious plan to deepen his faith and to dramatically move Job toward a trust in the LORD that is unconditional.

In these last verses of Job that make up the epilogue, we will make note of how the writer ties up all the themes established in the prologue. The issues of integrity, intercession, and blessing are neatly drawn to conclusions.

Not all ironic details have yet come out in the story, nor will they (as far as we know) prior to its being recorded. We have observed that Job's theology and worship has grown. But where do things stand regarding the challenges of *Satan* or the friends? Job has confessed sin. Did that confession show him a liar in his defense of his integrity? Did Satan have it right? Did the friends?

In this last chapter, we will be given certainty about these things. God will through direct speech or through his inspired writer provide information for us to draw conclusions about whether Job stands vindicated against his visible human opponents and or the invisible adversary.

Job's Integrity Vindicated by the LORD

Having accomplished his work in humbling Job and deepening his devotion, God now turns his attention to Eliphaz and the other friends.

> **Job 42:7–9**
> **7** After the LORD had finished speaking to Job, he said to Eliphaz the Temanite, "I am angry with you and your two friends, for you have not spoken the truth about me, as my servant Job has. **8** Now take seven bulls and seven rams, go to my servant Job, and offer a burnt offering for yourselves. Then my servant Job will pray for you. I will surely accept his prayer and not deal with you as your folly deserves. For you have not spoken the truth about me, as my servant Job has." **9** Then Eliphaz the Temanite, Bildad the Shuhite, and Zophar the Naamathite went and did as the LORD had told them, and the LORD accepted Job's prayer.

God publicly assessed Job twice before the heavenly council and the adversary (1:8 and 2:3). Now he does so on earth before the friends. In all cases, the assessments are positive. Let's consider

Job: The Cry of the Righteous Sufferer

this last scoresheet, and then we will see what ties there are between those of the prologue and this one of the epilogue.

First, there is an implication. God says he is angry with the friends and so implies he is *not* so with Job. The friends repeatedly asserted that Job was due God's wrath because of some sin he had committed, yet here is God declaring that it is *them* with whom he is angry. In fact, the friends must be shocked to find that Job is the only one standing *between* them and God's wrath! In giving his reason for this reversal, God gives a direct assertion that he is pleased with Job. Job has spoken the truth about God while the friends have not. Next, we observe that only Job is referred to as God's servant, which the context reveals as a blessed relationship. There is clearly a disposition of good will from God toward Job, and this is furthered by God's willingness to receive prayers of intercession from him.

These assessments have mutually exclusive implications for Job and the friends. Job is vindicated as the friends are rebuked. This means our conclusions in the last lesson are verified. Job's repentance was in regard to his reactions to his suffering but not in regard to any sin that the friends supposed had caused it. Job had remained wholeheartedly devoted to the LORD, despite speaking the words he later rejected. He was truly a righteous sufferer. Mark Job as vindicated on that count.

Further, consider the charge of Satan in chs.1-2. It was that if God will allow Job to suffer, then he "will surely curse you to your face" (1:11; 2:4). Job has not cursed God at all. He explicitly rejected his wife's recommendation to do so (2:9) and he has not done so in all his arguments with his friends. When presented in chs.38-42 with the opportunity to literally curse God to his face, Job did the opposite. He humbled himself, reaffirmed and deepened his commitment to worship and serve the LORD no matter what. God has vindicated Job on that count too. What's more, God has vindicated himself. His sovereign rule is shown to be generous and gracious and just, and no one has the authority or power to challenge it.

"...the truth about me..."

So, how are we to understand what is meant by this double-edged assessment that the three friends have not spoken the truth about God while Job has? The four men – and throw in Elihu to make it five – have agreed about God's great power, his mercy and his justice. They have all spoken truth about God. What is this specific truth that is voiced by Job and not the others? It must surely be important, for God references it twice, providing a bookend to vv.7-8. The men have clearly not spoken the truth about Job, but how have they failed to speak the truth about God?

What do you think God means here? What truth has Job spoken about God that the friends have not?

Job's Integrity, Intercession and Greater Blessing

First, we have two logical options about what is meant by God's statement regarding the friends. He may mean that the friends have spoken *untruth* about him, or he may mean they have *failed* to speak the truth about him. Have they been wrong, or have they been neglectful? The term "folly" contributes to the discussion. These men have said a lot about God judging the folly of the wicked, but now God attributes it to them. This could tip us toward their speaking untruth. Another question may be helpful. Why does God not mention Elihu?

The arguments of the friends were wordy but not sophisticated. Their retribution theology came out in simple form: *Job, your suffering must indicate that you have sinned*. The logical argument would look something like this:

> Premise 1: God is just.
> Premise 2: Justice demands that God bless righteousness and punish wickedness.
> Premise 3: Suffering is due to punishment.
> Premise 4: Job was suffering.
> Conclusion: Therefore, Job was being punished for wickedness.

We have already explored some of the deficiencies of the above theology. It does not allow for God's merciful generosity to freely bring temporary and earthly blessing upon even the wicked. It makes God the genie-in-a-bottle, servant of strict justice. Proponents assume they can commit even one truly righteous act and demand blessing from God. This puts them in the driver's seat. However, this is not possible, for it is God's character that defines righteousness and not ours. So, apart from God's generosity there could not be blessing, because even in doing right our motive (to get blessing) is corrupt and we are not truly righteous.

Job's arguments refuted the conclusion above, because he knew Premise 3 (suffering is due to punishment) was wrong in his case. He did not know why he was suffering, but he contended there must be some other Premise that would explain his suffering with a different conclusion.

Elihu also spoke toward that possibility. His arguments rose above those of the friends, allowing that suffering may have other purposes besides retribution. God may use it for *instruction* (36:15). Further, though Elihu doesn't seem to be aware of the depth of his own suggestion, God may use suffering for *rescue*. We understand from the NT perspective that the suffering of Christ accomplished exactly that. So, Elihu and Job somewhat blindly offer an expanded, more complex argument. To that above, they would modify and insert like thus:

> Premise 3a: Suffering *may be* due to punishment.
> Premise 3b: Suffering may be also allowed by God for other purposes.

With these additions, another conclusion is suitable:

> Conclusion 2: Job may be suffering for purposes unknown to Job and his friends.

Job: The Cry of the Righteous Sufferer

If Elihu was at all on the right track in his openness to unknown possibilities, that would explain why God does not rebuke him. Still, what truth did Job speak that the friends – in their folly – did NOT say? It seems bound up in what Job said in v.3:

> You asked, "Who is this who conceals my counsel with ignorance?"
> Surely I spoke about things I did not understand,
> things too wondrous for me to know.

Job recalls God's question, and then gives a direct answer: "I spoke about things too wondrous for me to know." The friends have never confessed this. They have only spoken from their rigid theological framework, as though they DO know everything about how God brings his justice to bear on the universe.

From that puny, earthly perspective they have condemned their friend, but worse, they have shrunk down the LORD. They have made Yahweh a mere courier for delivering justice rather than a Sovereign LORD who always works every kind of suffering according to his just purposes. Who else could take the free evil choices of the wicked (or satanic) and work them out for the good of the faithful? Think of how offensive the friends' low view of his sovereignty must have been to the Almighty! And of this they have not repented.

"...my servant Job..."
Twice in the prologue the LORD called Job his servant. Now, in the epilogue, he uses this term four times. In both contexts, the association is positive. Job's integrity as a faithful servant has been not only vindicated but amplified.

How is the LORD's repeated use of this term connected to Job's humbling by the LORD?

How is it connected to Job's blessing by the LORD?

Job's Intercession for His Friends
Just as Job's integrity has been vindicated, so too has the theme of intercession been advanced from prologue to epilogue. In ch.1, Job had interceded for his children (vv.5-6). In his times of intense suffering, Job has cried out for his own mediator to intercede for him (9:32-35). Further, he has put his hope in his Redeemer who alone can make things right (19:25).

Job's Integrity, Intercession and Greater Blessing

Now, the story has come full circle as Job's craving is affirmed by God. God installs Job to intercede for his friends through prayer. Job can only pray for them, but he cannot make things right. He can model God's forgiveness with his own, but he cannot atone for their folly. That must come through substitutionary sacrifice (42:8).

The friends follow God's prescription. Job shows his quality in forgiving and praying. God accepts the offering and the intercessory prayer.

How does the conclusion of this story amplify the gospel truths of Christ's intercession and his atoning sacrifice to provide forgiveness for sins?

Job's Greater Blessing

The major themes of this book have been amplified and tied up. One remains: Job's blessing. This too is amplified as Job's full life is doubly blessed:

> **10** After Job had prayed for his friends, the LORD restored his fortunes and doubled his previous possessions. **11** All his brothers, sisters, and former acquaintances came to him and dined with him in his house. They sympathized with him and comforted him concerning all the adversity the LORD had brought on him. Each one gave him a piece of silver and a gold earring.
>
> **12** So the LORD blessed the last part of Job's life more than the first. He owned fourteen thousand sheep and goats, six thousand camels, one thousand yoke of oxen, and one thousand female donkeys. **13** He also had seven sons and three daughters. **14** He named his first daughter Jemimah, his second Keziah, and his third Keren-happuch. **15** No women as beautiful as Job's daughters could be found in all the land, and their father granted them an inheritance with their brothers.
>
> **16** Job lived 140 years after this and saw his children and their children to the fourth generation. **17** Then Job died, old and full of days.

Job's restoration is total. He has been restored *spiritually* by God's presence and vindication. He is restored *socially* and *emotionally* (v.11) as well as *materially* (v.12). He is blessed with more children (v.13). He is apparently restored to health as he is granted long life (vv.16-17). The remarkable beauty of his daughters seems intended to augment the beauty of his blessed life. His granting them an inheritance is such a rarity (the only other biblical example is Nu 27) that it certainly reflects upon his great wealth. Further, it may represent the truth that God's blessings transcend human distinctions and are available to all. Job's longevity would also mean that his testimony of blessedness would have endured to generations with whom he could brag on God firsthand.

We should not overlook that God restores Job's blessings only *after* both his repentance and his mediation for his friends. The latter indicated his integrity in the former. His satisfaction in God resulted in true forgiveness of his friends. The necessity of forgiveness to receive blessing is affirmed by Jesus in his model prayer for his disciples, something we should not quickly forget:

> **Matthew 6:12–15**
> **12** And forgive us our debts,
> as we also have forgiven our debtors.
> **13** And do not bring us into temptation,
> but deliver us from the evil one.
> **14** "For if you forgive others their offenses, your heavenly Father will forgive you as well.
> **15** But if you don't forgive others, your Father will not forgive your offenses.

What do we make of the remarkably blessed state of Job's ending? It certainly is no affirmation of the retribution theology of the friends but rather an expression of God's generous grace. God is not bound to keep Job in his misery in order to prove retribution theology wrong. Neither is he bound to restore Job's blessing just to vindicate him against the accusations of his friends. God's perfectly wise and just rule is not undermined in the least by the accusations of Satan, by the wrongheadedness of the friends, nor by the confused angst of Job, rattled as he was for a time. God owes no creature anything. Still, while Job's restored blessing is not *compulsory* for God, it is *appropriate* and in keeping with his generous character. If God freely blesses even the unrighteous (for a time) – and he surely and evidently does – then how much more freely would he bless his faithful servant? So, while God is not *bound* to restore Job's blessing, it is certainly appropriate that he does.

At the end of this remarkable story, we can see that it makes an important contribution to the biblical theology of God and man. In it we see that God is absolutely sovereign, all-knowing, all-powerful, perfectly loving, and generous. By contrast, we see that we are creatures of dust, dependent, finite, flawed, and ignorant of the many lofty considerations that factor into God's perfect rule. In spite of this ignorance, and especially in the face of suffering, we can find peace, comfort and confidence in our God, if we will humbly cling to him and trust his generous love for us. Especially now that Christ has come, we can confidently assert with Job that our Redeemer lives, and we can long for the day that our eyes will look upon him, and not as a stranger but as a merciful Savior.

Job's Integrity, Intercession and Greater Blessing

Reflection Upon the Lessons from Job
As we conclude our study of Job, the righteous sufferer, we have much that we can apply to our own situations and seasons of suffering. We may also be better equipped to minister to others in such seasons of their own. Here are some suggested applications:

Count your blessings.
If you were in Job's shoes, what blessings could you name off in your opening chapter?

Be aware of your enemy.
How can you be alert to the attacks of Satan? What is his goal in those attacks?

Don't be disappointed by your friends.
How can you receive encouragement from others when things go wrong? Why should you be careful to have limited expectations of that help? What have you learned about offering that help?

Take inventory in your suffering.
Since suffering may come for several reasons, how should you examine yourself when it does come?

Learn and grow in your suffering.
Whatever the cause of your suffering, how can you count it as joy and be matured through it (Jas 1:2-4)?

Trust God in your suffering.
What practical things can you do to strengthen your faith, or that of others in these times?

Job: The Cry of the Righteous Sufferer

Meditate on the gospel blessings of Jesus who suffered to bring you blessing.
For final reflection, how is Jesus the perfect fulfillment of 1) a man of perfect integrity, 2) a righteous man who suffered for cosmic reasons, 3) a mediator and 4) a redeemer? How does Scripture reveal him as the Creator, the sovereign LORD who perfectly and justly rules the universe and works all things for the good of those he calls?

Proverbs 10:24–25
What the wicked dreads will come to him,
but what the righteous desire will be given to them.
When the whirlwind passes,
the wicked are no more,
but the righteous are secure forever.

It Is Well with My Soul
When peace like a river attendeth my way
When sorrows like sea billows roll
Whatever my lot, Thou hast taught me to say
It is well, it is well with my soul

It is well with my soul
It is well, it is well with my soul

Tho' Satan should buffet, tho' trials should come
Let this blest assurance control:
That Christ hath regarded my helpless estate
And hath shed his own blood for my soul

My sin, O the bliss of this glorious tho't
My sin, not in part but the whole
Is nailed to the cross and I bear it no more
Praise the Lord, praise the Lord, O my soul

And Lord haste the day when my faith shall be sight
The clouds be rolled back as a scroll
The trump shall resound, and the Lord shall descend
Even so, it is well with my soul

It is well with my soul
It is well, it is well with my soul

About the Author

Benjamin Gum holds a Master of Theological Studies degree from Midwestern Baptist Theological Seminary (MBTS). He blogs at bengum.blogspot.com. He is also a musician and songwriter. Gum has been in vocational ministry for over 30 years, serving as pastor, teacher, worship leader, music teacher, and small group leader, among other things. He currently serves as a pastor in the western suburbs of Kansas City and continues to write worship songs for the church. Benjamin and his wife, Dawna, have four adult children and twelve grandchildren. They have also fostered nearly ninety boys.

Check out his other Bible study workbooks:

Revelation: A Journey through the Apocalypse Guided by Its Purpose, Function and Goal

Hebrews: The Superior Savior and the Exhortation to Endure.

Gum has also written a basic discipleship resource, **Making Disciples**, as well as a challenge for church worship leaders, **Skinny Jeans Fat Shoes**.

www.ingramcontent.com/pod-product-compliance
Lightning Source LLC
LaVergne TN
LVHW061253060426
835507LV00020B/2309